Anne M Carson

Anne M Carson is a writer and visual artist from Melbourne, Australia, who has published four collections of poetry, and has been published in literary journals in Australia and internationally. She has won and been commended in numerous poetry prizes including short-listing in the inaugural 2015 Ron Pretty Poetry Prize. She has curated two programs for Australia's National Poetry Program PoeticA and hosted a series of poetry and music soirées, including a range of poetry-led experiments in social activism. These have included *The River Soiree on Herring Island*, which raised funds for the *Melbourne River Keepers*. In 2014 she conducted the *SecondBite Poetry Prize* which raised funds for *SecondBite*, the food rescue and redistribution charity. In 2017 she donated the modern epic poem *Writing on the Wall* as a fundraiser for Anti-Slavery Australia. She is Director Arts for Ondru, the social-change-through-the-arts organisation.

As a creative writing therapist she has edited and facilitated the group process which has resulted in the publication of three books. She has taught Poetry Writing and Appreciation to adults and is a trained social worker. Her visual art is based on photography and botanical specimens and her photographs and art panels have been exhibited in galleries, florist shops and used as greeting cards, a bookmark and a literary journal cover.

www.annemcarson.com

Also by Anne M Carson

Poetry

Writing on the Wall

Removing the Kimono

Two Green Parrots

As Editor

The Sounds of Colour: The stories of mothers of and workers with children on the Autism Spectrum

Kaleidoscope, Autism through the Eyes of Mothers

Espresso Chapbook

Choices From the Heart: A Collection of Stories

Massaging Himmler

A Poetic Biography of Dr Felix Kersten

Anne M Carson

HYBRID
PUBLISHERS

Published by Hybrid Publishers

Melbourne Victoria Australia

© Anne M. Carson 2019

This publication is copyright. Apart from any use
as permitted under the Copyright Act 1968, no part may be reproduced
by any process without prior written permission from the publisher.
Requests and enquiries concerning reproduction
should be addressed to the Publisher,
Hybrid Publishers,
PO Box 52, Ormond, VIC Australia 3204.

www.hybridpublishers.com.au

First published 2019

A catalogue record for this
book is available from the
National Library of Australia

ISBN 9781925736199 (p)
9781925736403 (e)

Cover design: Joanne Marchese

Photos with kind permission from the family collection of Arno Kersten

Acknowledgements

I would like to thank the editors of the following journals for publishing my poems, sometimes in slightly different versions:

- "Elisabeth Lüben opens her heart", *Eureka Street*, August, 2010
- "Felix wants them to have suffered", *Melbourne PEN Newsletter*, 2010
- "Felix has lunch with Mussolini: a rhapsody in four courses", *Cordite* 37, 2011
- "Dr Ko explains sky burial", *Cordite* 40, 2012
- "The librarian witnesses the burning", *Eureka Street*, 2012
- "Felix contemplates the fall of France", *Paris Literary Review*, April 2016
- "Felix hears more bad news", *Paris Literary Review*, April 2016
- "Time of death: April 16, 1960", *Paris Literary Review*, 200, April 2016
- "Felix has some modest success", *The Journal*, 46 (UK), 2016
- "Felix returns to the fray", *The Journal*, 46 (UK), 2016
- "Of the 2,700: one voice", *Southerly*, 75:3, 2016
- "Schellenberg warns Felix", *Live Encounters in Poetry and Writing*, March 2017
- "Felix shakes for hours", *Live Encounters in Poetry and Writing*, March 2017

Massaging Himmler:
A Poetic Biography of Dr Felix Kersten

"See with a feeling eye, feel with a seeing hand."
>   – Goethe, *Roman Elegies* quoted by Dr Felix Kersten

"The world today is a sick world, and it was made so by a group of sick men, many of whom were under my medical care during the war years."
>   – Dr Felix Kersten, 1947

"And so we must know these good people who helped Jews during the Holocaust. We must learn from them, and in gratitude and hope, we must remember them."
>   – Elie Wiesel

Dedicated with deep thanks to my partner Julian Bailey and dear friend Alison Elliott – neither seemed to tire of all manner of Kersten-related discussions, or flag in their belief in me or the project. Blessed to have such loyal, loving supporters.

This work is an imaginative reconstruction of Dr Felix Kersten's story. I have imagined the inner lives of the characters, their conversations and daily life, in and around the known facts. In the case of conversations, I have blended real and imagined in the text, but provided references at the back of the book for all quotes so those who want to learn more of the story can follow the trail.

Felix's background – education – early experiences – deciding
to become a masseur – meeting and studying under Dr Ko. Dr Ko
describes his prophecy – style of healing – spirituality. Dr Ko returns
to Tibet. Felix assumes Dr Ko's healing practice. Various clients give
testimonials – the Nazis come to power – Dr Ko dies.

Felix grieves Dr Ko – notices changes in Germany – explains his work,
his loneliness – meets his future wife – talks about his philosophy
– buys his Heartworld. Himmler talks about the Blood Purge – the
Cathedral of Light – his success – his daughter. Kristallnacht. More
testimonies for Felix. Felix's first meeting with Himmler. Himmler in
pain – at table. Germany's military action increases – Felix wonders
if they are safe at Scheveningen.

Felix and Irmgard move to Hartzwalde. Himmler flexes his control.
Felix secures his first release – sets up his underground – deals with
Himmler's control and rage – discovers Himmler's plans for the Dutch
– learns to manipulate Himmler. The Nazis begin systematic killing of
Jews. Felix is horrified about Himmler's attitudes. Felix's father dies.

Himmler 'justifies' his anti-Semitism. Felix and Irmgard give refuge
to Jehovah's Witnesses – are horrified by concentration camps. Felix
resolves to do more – joins forces with Schellenberg – accompanies
Himmler to Finland – is asked to treat the Führer – secures more
releases – realises he has to get his family out. Irmgard gives birth.
Elisabeth supports Felix – keeps a tally of releases.

Felix helps the Swedish Government's White Bus scheme – finds a house to rent in Stockholm – continues to treat Himmler – manipulates him to release more prisoners – hears about the attack on Hitler – almost dies in an ambush – harbours his collaborator – moves his family to Sweden – works internationally on release schemes. Irmgard helps Felix. Elisabeth describes Felix's gastronomy. A poem in the name of released prisoners.

Felix continues to work for peace – secures more releases – succeeds in stopping Himmler bombing The Hague – works on the White Bus scheme – finds Himmler impossible to work with – decides to host a meeting with Himmler and representative of World Jewish Congress – hosts the most unlikely meeting in history – describes the end of the war – resettles in Sweden – has difficulty being granted Swedish citizenship. Himmler dies. A poem in the name of the released.

PROLOGUE

Felix talks about snakes beneath the bed
National Socialist Headquarters, Chancellery, Berlin, 1939

Think physiotherapy, massage – clinical,
white-sheet words, washed hands, nails

nicely groomed. The bed is made up,
white sterilised towels, cotton coverlet.

Anodyne atmosphere, hushed voices,
healing hands – no place for passion,

poison. His bed is a divan pressed up against
the wall. A dark room with solid wooden

furniture. Woollen blankets are brown as
boot polish. Spartan, masculine, he sleeps

here between duties when he cannot make it
home or to his mistress. Or when his guts

are so badly spasmed it is all he can do to
stay conscious, maintain his grip on the reins

of power. I don a white treatment coat but
may as well not bother for all the protection

it offers: beneath the bed is a nest of vipers –
venomous, virile. They breed so quickly,

hundreds of hatchlings, scores of adults
in a medusa mess. They writhe and gripe,

twine round the bed legs, slither up to me
fangs out, tasting air. You think this is metaphor?

CHAPTER I

1   Felix describes his inheritance
Helsinki, Finland, 1919

Mutti had the touch. She had it from her Mutti
who had it from hers – hands that healed, held

over hurt – bone-setting, taking the heat out
of rheumatic joints, sprains and muscle tears.

A family gift passed down for generations
through the female line. In Northern countries

massage is just a normal part of life – an old
respected art. Few doctors work the countryside,

so women like my Mutti are the ones who heal.
She passed it on to me. Unusual in a male but

ever since I was a boy I knew my hands were
wise. Sensitive, I could not bear to have them

soiled or rasped. Not delicate to look at – large
palms, short squat fingers. Despite their size

and heft, the kids still called me sissy.
But it was me they asked to soothe the skittish

milkers, mares in labour. I inherited Mutti's
hands, her knack – the magic gift of healing.

28 June 1919

Versailles Treaty

The Treaty
is ratified by
Germany,
reparations to be
decided. The Nazi
Party rejects the
Treaty.

2   Felix learns the value of hard work
1920

I am born in 1898 in Yuriev, a Baltic town
in Czarist Russia. Well-to-do, an only child.

Boyhood filled with pleasure; skating
and sled rides in winter, singing, eating

of course, and Finnish seaside summer holidays.
Indulged at least until I am seven when Vater

sends me off to boarding school. Five years
meant to toughen me up so I will apply myself

but I only just scrape through despite repeated
warnings. Early in '14, the first war nipping

Europe's heels, he sends me further away
to Agricultural College in Germany.

The Czarists have grown distrustful of people
of German stock like Mutti and Vati and they

are banished to a tiny Caspian Sea town
in Turkestan. Devastation! Only sixteen –

suddenly I need make my own way. No letters
or food parcels, no pocket money, or presents,

no-one to turn to for support, for affection
or care! Only then do I understand Vati's

insistence on hard work. Almost overnight I
change, begin to knuckle down and take life

seriously. I never would have said so at the time,
but that early hardship is my making.

3 Felix talks about his flair for languages
Military hospital, Helsinki, 1920

Languages have always been my forte. We speak
Russian at home as well as German because

of Vati's nationality. Then Latvian while boarding
at secondary school in Riga. Later I study Agriculture

in Germany. The authorities consider me a subject
of William II because I have a German father. They

want me to fight the Russians with them but I grew up
in Czarist Russia and have no heart for it. I join

the Finnish German legion instead, fighting for
independence of the Baltic States. There in the Guards,

I learn Finnish. By the time my column marches into
Estonia in '19, I have made Officer. We arrive in Yuriev,

my home town, its old name Dorpat restored.
Returned from exile my dear parents greet me.

How joyful our reunion! A chance to taste favourite
Mutti-cooked meals, to bask as much-loved son.

A short and happy sojourn before war claims me again
and my regiment is on the move. Russian troops

catch us in the marshes without any kind of shelter
for a whole miserable winter. The cold and damp

creep into my limbs and rheumatism cripples me.
Slowly, painfully, I limp on crutches into the hospital

here for treatment. Time to reflect on my future.
Who am I, where do I belong? A mix of cultures,

languages … I do not identify with only one.
But Finland has been good to me, has coaxed me

back to health. Thanks to her excellent physicians,
my legs daily grow stronger. This decides me –

Munich,
Germany, 1920

The Deutsche
Arbeiterpartei
(1919) becomes
the National-
sozialistische
Deutsche
Arbeitpartei or
NSDP (Nazi
Party). Strongly
nationalisitic,
fundamentally
anti-Semitic,
it adheres to a
racial ideology.
The NSDAP often
characterises
capitalism, high
finance and
big business
as 'Jewish'. It
seeks to draw
workers away
from Communism
to 'National
Socialism'.
Realising early
the value of
propaganda, the
Nazi Party buys
its first newspaper
the *Völkischer
Beobachter*
[People's
Observer] in 1920,
the year the Party
is formed.
The Party adopts
the swastika as
a symbol of the
Aryan race.

I will become a Finnish citizen. Grateful for their care,
but more important, in a world grown violent and bloody-

minded, I admire her military neutrality. Perhaps becoming
hers will keep me safe from soldierly demands.

4   Felix lands on his feet
The Lübens' apartment, Berlin, 1921

This year I complete my Finnish Diploma in Scientific
Massage, have come to the German capital to try

my luck. I need more study, natürlich, and am enrolled
in the Faculty where staff tell me I will make an excellent

masseur. I lodge with the Lübens, mother and daughter,
in their apartment. Family friends and I have fitted right

in. They fuss over me – I never expected to find myself
two Muttis so far from home! After active service,

learning to use my legs again in hospital, I know I cannot
remain a military man – enough bloodshed to last

a whole life. All my Vati's holdings have been swallowed
in Estonia's agrarian reforms. So there is no family land

where I can practise my agricultural skills. What am I
to do? Recovering in Helsinki I witness the doctors'

expertise, the lives they save. Perhaps I can be a
surgeon? But when I confide to Major Eckman, the

hospital's head doctor, he says: "See your fleshy, strong
palm, the broad short fingers. This hand is perfect for

massage, and much less suitable for surgery. And the
training is shorter." He knows my meagre resources,

immediately puts me to work, learning while I help
the hospital masseurs. Thrilling to find a way to use my

childhood talent. How I love the work! Like Mutti,
my hands just seem to know where to find the knot,

how to winkle it out. So much joy to see the fire of pain
desert a soldier's eyes, witness his calm return. Patients

ask for me over the qualified masseurs. I have taken my
doctor's advice, decide to pursue a career in massage.

Words from the
Nazi lexicon,
Germany, 1920s

Blut und Boden
(Blood and Soil)

An ideal adopted
by the Nazis.
It describes a
'back to the
land' approach
to combat
the perceived
rootlessness of
modern industrial
life and also the
idea that German
land was bound,
almost mystically,
to German blood.
Peasants became
Nazi cultural
heroes, guardians
of German racial
stock and German
history.

5   Felix describes his worst massage
Berlin, 1922

Professor Bier from the school where I study
introduced me this week to a fascinating

Tibetan monk, a practitioner of Oriental healing
arts. Saffron robes and the kindest face, shining

eyes. He suggests I demonstrate Finnish
massage – on him! When finished I prepare

to receive compliments, as is common from
my teachers. I have given a truly excellent

massage; national pride for our treatment
to measure up to his. Oh, he is polite enough,

but says I know nothing, absolutely nothing!
I am flabbergasted. Then he says I am the one

he has come halfway round the world to find.
That his horoscope spelled out this very meeting

and I am the very man! My head is reeling,
I do not know what to think … But there is

something intriguing about him, inclining me
towards trust … I decide on the spot to study

under him – *disciple* is the word he uses.
What does he mean? We have made an

appointment for my first lesson. Time will tell
just exactly in what I have myself involved.

6   Felix explains the Finnish Crown Affair

Helsinki, 1922

I could not help myself – a touch of class, cachet
with the Fräulein. I had my visiting-card embossed

with a royal crown – to lend distinction! Not that
there is royalty in Finland but the country is loud

with nobles. Count this, Contessa that. A crown
to grace my dreams, 'Count Kersten' has the right

degree of gravitas, the proper weight … where is
the harm? It was just a bit of fun, a folly followed

by a summons in the post. Chalk it to experience,
though I hope Dr Ko never gets to know. I have not

yet uncovered who turned me in – many envy
me my luck. The Court said I had no right but

it will not be long before I find my proper place.
Meantime I am happy to accept the blame, pay

the fine. Sometimes I bemoan my fate – the soul
of a nobleman … trapped in the body of a burgher.

1921

**Versailles
Reparations**

Germany agrees
to pay 6.6 billion
pounds, although
it is unclear if she
actually can.
Adolf Hitler
becomes leader
of the Nazi
Party and the
Sturmabteilung
(SA storm troopers
or Brownshirts)
are founded as a
party militia. They
begin immediate
violent attacks on
other parties.

7   Dr Ko talks of prophecy
Berlin, 1922

My chart was drawn when I first put on monk
robes back in the 1800s. Tibetan astrologers

are seers – they peer into future – pass through
barrier of time. Their prophecy for me: in 1922

you meet young man who knows nothing, you
teach him everything! I did not know what it

meant but it has come to pass. In Tibet, after all,
we take view that time is elastic. My master,

he specialise in massage, so careful with me,
patient. He guides study of Sowa Rigpa –

science of Tibetan healing. He lives Buddhist
teachings, showers me with love, compassion,

understanding. Everyone call him *Rinpoche* –
Precious One. He is our *Gompa*'s Lama-doctor –

villagers, nomads come for kind hands, strong
medicine. He takes me through Medicine *Sutras*,

supervise my practice. Meditation – so important
to train mind in equanimity, open river of

compassion. Vanity get whittled down. You not
heal when own self get in the way. I also study

Chinese medicine; wrist-pulse reading, listening
through fingerpads. Good doctors feel into body –

heat, cool, damp, block, flow – all, how you say?
correspondences. My master taught tracing-in of

sickness to fundamental cause, back out again to
symptom. Body and mind joined, both make health

or sickness. His mantra – balance is mother of this
art, health its child. And hands – deep into viscera –

direct manipulation of plex of nerves, treatment of
lymph and blood. Twenty years to master skill,

but I join two – Tibetan, Chinese – into one, become
adept. "Ready," says my *Rinpoche*. Next, prophecy

pulls me from *Gompa* in Land of Snows all the way
to London to study medicine in Western College.

My great privilege to be one of first monks to come
to West. How wide their eyes when they see

Buddhist robes in British streets! It makes me smile –
we are all humans underneath our clothes! Prophecy

leads me like a yak by nose, to Berlin where I
set up Medicine Practice. Patients search this healing

out – people are helped, word spreads. Cures don't
always come but often, others are happy for relief.

Just this week I was introduced to the man prophecy
prepared me for. Herr Felix Kersten he is called.

I know him straight away, ask him for Finnish massage.
Never so happy to have worthless treatment in my life!

After waiting, wondering, I cannot help myself –
I tell him: "I have waited for you – for thirty years!"

8   Felix describes learning under Dr Ko
Berlin, 1922

He is the kindest of tutors, but his teachings are strict
and they take a good while to master. Meditation

is the plinth on which all else rests. Whenever I am
not busy with my classes at the Faculty or working

my many jobs, we practise together to achieve single-
pointed concentration. I progress; every day I go

deeper, stay absorbed longer. A whole-life approach
– no imbibing of alcohol or other stimulants. But

Dr Ko permits the enjoyment of food, in plenty;
he cooks for me, delicious dishes from his homeland

– *momos* my favourite! And – he considers physical
relations with women salutary – to balance the nerves.

9 Felix observes his city

Berlin,1922

Berlin is changing. The Nazis
have hung huge banners over

the faces of public buildings,
big enough to penetrate even

my apolitical blinkers. They are
loud additions to the dull greys

and pinched monochromes
of a suffering city. The hungry

Volk love them and are heartened.
They rouse the spirits like

brave rouge on a sick woman's
cheeks. Such bold promises

of optimism. Swastikas bloom
blood-red amid the gloom.

10 A postikortti from Felix
Berlin, September 1922

Rakkaani,

I will be visiting Helsinki on Sept 21st and would love
to see you. Would you come to my hotel at 8 pm for
supper? I will let the doorman know to expect you.

Rakkaus,
Felix

11 A lecture by Dr Ko
Akademie für Medizin, Berlin, 1922

Sang.gyä ch'ö.dang tsog.kyi ch'og.nam.la,
J'ang.ch'ub bar.d'u dag.ni kyab.su.ch'I,
Dag.g'I jin..sog gyi.päö so.nam.kyi,
Dro.la pan.ch'ir sang.gyädrub.par.shog.

Let me translate for you: Until I am
enlightened, I go for refuge to triple gem –
Buddha, Dharma, Sangha. Through

virtue I make by practising giving and
other perfections, may I become Buddha
to benefit sentient beings.

*

There is a lot of suffering in the world – isn't it?
What this prayer means is that Buddhists want
to help beings who suffer – our job as doctors

too – we take Hippocratic vow. Already, Freunde,
before I even start talking and though I dress
different – we have much in common! It makes

me happy to talk with you tonight on things dear
to me – marriage of East and West teachings in
my work. I have great good fortune – both Tibetan

and Chinese Masters. I learn to listen to body
through fingerpads. So sensitive – like very, very
fine radar even slightest movement they pick up.

As well, from my Master, *Rinpoche*, mind-training,
meditation. That single-pointed concentration –
we call *Varja* concentration, clear and sharp like

diamond – I see something like on face of surgeon
when he operate. I travel to Britain, study in London
Medical School, learn word 'proprioception' – this

is very clever – body is very clever – isn't it? It knows
where are its parts, next to other parts. Perfect
example of what Western science good at – it tells me

category, method for my most cherished massage
skill! Stretch receptors – isn't it? – in muscles and
tendons tell brain about body movement. This is

physiologic feedback mechanism. Add meditation
to proprioception and extraordinary thing happens.
External detail falls away. Gone – awareness of clock

tick-ticking down hall, rain hitting window pane.
Even rise and fall of own chest as it breathes. Focus
only on what fingerpads feel from body underneath

hand. Meditation goes deeper, perception of
movement amplified – what is minuscule becomes –
how you say – vast. Ordinary mind – he can hardly

feel a thing but under proprioception in meditation,
whole new symphony – movement of lymph and
blood along vessels is like music; swell, ebb, swell

again. That's what pulses feel like under healing
hand. Lama-doctors use this body-music for diagnosis.
Other things help – texture, temperature, degree of

pressure – but proprioception is key. Tibet and China
have much ancient knowledge – we call it *Sowa Rigpa* –
Science of Healing. The West has modern method,

scientific names, experiments that prove. Together
we have much cooperation, learning. Danke schön.
Om Mani Peme Hung. Om Mani Peme Hung.

12 Dr Ko talks about his meditation mat
Berlin, 1923

Now I go so far from home – my rug is
anchor, tethers me to vows and prayers,
connects me to *Sangha* in Tibet. No larger

than chair-seat, but powerful meditation
medicine. Double *Dorje* pattern – diamond
and thunderbolt for determination. As soon

as I sit, I remember monastery – meditation
hall, loud, boom-boom of chanting monks.
Mat says *Bodhisattva*, reminds me to help

other beings be free from suffering, causes
of suffering. I wish, repeat my wish tens of
thousands of times in prayer, cross-legged

on rug. My prayer enters mat. My mat grows
full of prayer. Monks let things go, every
day practise detachment from things.

I know it is not Buddhist way, my *Rinpoche*
would scold me. But I am far from home –
I grasp meditation mat – and not let go!

Germany, 1923

The Ruhr Crisis
Germany fails this
year's reparation
repayment – a
consignment of
timber. France
and Belgium
invade the
Ruhr, leading to
hyperinflation;
banknotes now
worth less than
lumps of coal.
Strikes and the
resignation of
the Government
follow, and the
Communist Party
(KPD) prepares
for revolution.
Radical and
revolutionary
right-wing politics
also expands
and Nazi Party
membership
swells to 20,000.

Germany, 1923

***Bürgerbräukeller-Putsch* (The Beer Hall Putsch)**

Staged by the Nazi Party in an attempt to gain power. It fails and the Party is banned. Hitler is arrested, tried for treason in 1924 and imprisoned in Landsberg prison near Munich. He dictates *Mein Kampf* (My Struggle) to his loyal aide Rudolf Hess, whilst in jail, and is released later the same year.

13 Dr Ko's patient gives a testimonial
Berlin, 1923

He empties his hands, shaking off
the imprint of others before me, static
snapping like wing feathers on an updraft.

Then he cups the bony ball my skull makes –
my whole world's globe cradled in his hands.
Hard to fathom how much I trust this.

Spinal fluid descends the dark tunnel –
the body's sap rising and falling – rising
again to hydrate hemispheres.

His art is to decipher the game pulse plays,
to sense the jam or float of sutures where skull
plates meet, to help the pulse travel free

to body's edge. His hands are fine enough to
read meninges, taut or loose those membranes
wrapping the brain in protective clothing

the way uterus enfolds foetus.
We are more music than hydraulic, more
symphonic. His hands nudge me through

melody into mystic. Slight the pressure,
profound the presence. Reaching the core,
sweetness from the bones.

14 Elisabeth Lüben opens her heart
The Lübens' apartment, Berlin, 1920s

Mutti treats Felix like one of her own. Naturally I help her
 out. I darn his socks, turn collars
 on his shirts, his cuffs as well.
 Occasionally he gets a bolt of cotton
 and the tailor runs up a few new shirts.
 Otherwise I am happy to cut and turn.

Small service when he works so hard. He takes every job
 he finds: dishwasher, longshoreman,
 interpreter – he even acts
 for the cinema!

I battle with myself about the diamond – Vati gave it to me
 just before he died. Small in carats
 but light from its facets
 shine as sweet as from any larger jewel.
 I could hardly admit it to myself
 but all my shy hopes lie hidden in that stone –
 home and hearth, a Mann who cares –
 Kinder, Küche, Kirche,
 they call it – socially sanctioned way.

Already I can see the setting I would choose, the sparkle
 of it on my hand. Then I notice
 Felix stuffing pages from
 the *Zeitung* into holes
 gaping in his shoes. Well, I need
 no persuasion to sell it then.

Still I wonder if he might ask me. Sitting quietly
 in the parlour – he says it soothes him
 to see me sew. The rustle of the cloth,
 punctuated by the pull of thread –
 how quiet it is between us!
 We need little beyond the sanctity
 of that brief time.

Germany, 1924

The Nazi Party contests federal elections for the first time – at first with little success but the party continues to grow. The Nazis strongly appeal to the lower middle-class who have suffered from the early 1920s inflation and fear Bolshevism the most. The small business class is receptive to Hitler's anti-Semitism, since they blame Jewish big business for their economic problems. University students also become a large constituency.

15 Felix farewells Dr Ko
Berlin, 1925

Exceptional, was how he described the sensitivity
of my hands after he had taught me, able to detect

the smallest movement of muscle, nerve. Perfectly
suited to massage, as my teachers before – Dr Kolander,

Professor Bier – had said. For three years I work hard,
mastering his technique and the single-pointed

meditation required. Do not get me wrong, I never
seek Nirvana – far too *in der Welt* for that. But

comes the day Tibet calls out to him across the years
of absence, the distance in between – the monastery

where he spent his middle years, the open sky and
nearby mountain range. His prophecy had spelled

it out: *when you teach him all he knows, you will
venture home, prepare for death* … He packs his bags,

leaves the following day. I never hear from him
again. Overnight life is revolutionised. He leaves

to me his healing art and, throughout Europe,
his entire paying clientele! Finally I have the means

to shape a decent life; the way I have always
wanted, nein, expected it to be … Truly it breaks

my heart. More than just the passing on of skill,
we meet in meditation – man to man, mind to mind;

mine to follow, his to lead. Special, precious bond
when you meditate with one proficient in the art.

They take you deeper than you could go alone,
awakening the wisdom-means of deep abiding –

initiates keep the ancient lineage alive. I know he
has to go but how I will miss his counsel, the vigour

of the talks we had on healing, meals we shared.
I must relinquish him – knowing profoundest debt.

**The reorganisation
of the Nazi Party**

Having failed
in their 1923
revolution, the
party is reorganised
under Hitler's
leadership to focus
on parliamentary-
political means
for gaining
power. This often
includes publicly
disavowing
violence, although
members of the
paramilitary units
(SA, SS) continue
to engage in
widespread
skirmishes,
particularly with
their largest rival,
the Communists.

16 Felix buys an Auto
Berlin, 1925

The first thing I do is buy an Auto which purrs – forget
the putt-putts, I want streamlined, sleek, a car that

oozes privilege, prestige. Must have grunt, muscle
beneath the bonnet. Leather seats and walnut dash,

timber steering-wheel, trim that shines, hubcaps
where you see your likeness. I cannot decide, Daimler

or Mercedes-Benz? Both *ausgezeichnet* machines.
The top brass drive the 770, black with tinted windows –

Grosse Mercedes if you're in the know – they really
know their Autos. The only other things I want for sure

are: épaulettes, some polished button-brass, white gloves
on the hands of the chauffeur, liveried, spelling luxury.

At last I have the means. I will buy the look, the life.
Pay others to care for manual necessities.

17 A Postkarte from Felix
Den Haag, Nederland, March 1926

Liebchen,

I will be in Berlin again in a month for my annual
season from the 24th. Would you grant me the
pleasure of your company at a small gathering at
the Eden Bar? Elisabeth will take a message at the
apartment.

Mit Liebe,
F

18 Elisabeth Lüben loves her job
Felix's apartment, Wilmersdorf, Berlin, 1927

I have now assisted Felix for a handful of happy years –
    first at Mutti's when he studied,
    then as housekeeper/secretary
    here in Wilmersdorf.

He engaged me when he bought this apartment after
    Dr Ko left. I stocked it with furniture,
    saw to all the requisites including
    furnishing my own rooms.

Large enough for a sitting room for me as well as
    bedroom. I like order
    and find I have an aptitude.
    Felix gives me plenty of scope!

He is much in demand and his reputation spreads.
    He informs me that his friend the Count
    is asking him to find rooms in Rome
    to add that city to his circuit.

Already patients wait a month to see him. He works only
    with those capable of total cure.
    Some protest – but it is his strictest
    rule. His charm (and my firmness)
    persuades them it is for the best.
    Five thousand marks is charged,
    but he sees non-paying clients too,
    humanitarian like Dr Ko.

I run his social calendar as well – he works so hard
    it is crucial he takes his leisure
    with friends at the end of the working day.
    I prepare supper so he can bring people
    back after the theatre.
    Sometimes he asks me to join them,
    or he calls me in to his private sitting room.
    I bring the coffee pot and a pastry;
    he tells me about his day.

19 Koningin Wilhelmina der Nederlanden gives a testimonial

Den Haag, Nederland, 1928

Doktor Kersten is recommended to us by friends
and I request his attendance at the Palace in Den Haag.

My husband, the Prince, is gravely ill, confined
to bed, too weak at times to lift his head.

Our doctors give him only six short months. Dr Kersten
consents to a consultation, uses his skill to boost

the nerves which feed the heart. My husband revives
– a miracle to see colour in his cheeks, him strong

enough to make a jest. He resumes his work, lives
a vibrant life, cherished consort to the Queen. We urge

Felix to make his home here in Den Haag. In honour
of his service, to secure his future aid, I appoint him

Hofarts – Physician to the Queen. Dutch by ancestry,
it pleases him to have won court favour. He sets up

residence, takes on further clientele – royal appointment
acts as imprimatur. We owe the greatest debt to Doktor

Felix Kersten – when hope of normal life was gone,
Hendrik survives, thrives – my husband and my Prince.

20 A briefkaart from Felix
Berlin, 1928

Lieve juffrouw,

We met at a soirée hosted by Mr and Mrs Bruin
and spent a pleasant time discussing illumination
in Flemish paintings – perhaps a shared passion?
Please join me for tea at the Hotel Rembrandt
during my forthcoming visit to Den Haag.

Met de beste wensen,
Dr Felix Kersten

21 Herr Rosterg gives a testimonial
Berlin, 1928

August Rosterg: industrialist, at your service. I own
multiple mines, extensive potassium works. Wealth

and considerable power are my reward – but the cost
has been extreme. My health is constantly harassed

– demands, decisions. It tells in migraines, exhaustion,
insomnia. How can you put a price on health?

When I first consult Herr Kersten he names his
standard fee – 5000 marks. Paltry, if he delivers.

Previous so-called cures and treatments offer only poor
relief. Nothing lasts until Felix lays his hands on me.

Digging deep, he says my nerves are shot. He works
me hard, agony to feel his hands wrench blockages

apart. Then back the next day for more of the same.
He treats me for several weeks. Eventually my innards

loosen up. He manages a total cure. The relief of sleeping
through the night – so many years of broken, fitful sleep

– of waking fresh and working the whole day through
without the tedium of ill-health. At the Wochenende

to have energy for family and social life! When I
come to write the cheque, I pen 100,000 marks.

22 Felix discovers his mistake
Berlin, 1928

What a fool! I catch only a glimpse of numbers
on the cheque Herr Rosterg gave me, notice the '1'

and think he has underpaid. Embarrassed that
a man so rich would come the miser when I effect

a total cure. They say he is worth 300,000 million
marks. But the teller says, "Doktor, you have omitted

two noughts on your paying-in slip." Sure enough
the cheque is made out for 100,000 marks! After years

of penury – scraping to make ends meet, the dishes
washed, the years of heavy labour at Helsinki Port …

Elisabeth advises me to buy some land. Sound advice
I think. I find the estate *Gut Hartzwalde*, just forty

miles east of Berlin, and immediately know it is for
me. My 'Heartworld' it will be. Here I will bring

my bride, raise a brood of children: 750 acres
on which to put my agricultural degree to use,

work the land – self-sufficiency my goal. Alongside
my residence in Den Haag, my apartment in Berlin,

I shall put deep roots down at Hartzwalde.
When the time arrives, it is here I will retire.

23 Dr Ko calls on the Wrathful Deities
Monastery, north-eastern Tibet, 1930

We could use the belching conch shell
now. We could do with the *suona* horn's
long blast of thunder, the metallic crash

of cymbals. We need drumbeats to
judder through our bones. We could use
cacophony – loud and lurid enough

to wake us, so we see what ripens
under our very nose, find strength to
prevail. If I could bring them bodily

from Tibet I would, a whole monastery
of monks, calling on the Wrathful
Deities to drive the dark forces away.

Berlin,
September 1930

The Nazis are no
longer a marginal
party, winning an
astonishing 107
seats out of 577 in
the Reichstag. By
October, the SA
engages in anti-
Jewish violence,
smashing the
windows of stores
on Potsdamer
Platz.

Berlin, 1931

"Joseph Goebbels,
Reich Propaganda
Minister, prepares
the crowd for
Hitler. Goebbels:
'Why do we trust
our Führer? …
We hold to our
Führer because
– he holds to us.'
A roar rose from
twenty thousand
throats …
Hitler began
speaking in his
odd, croaking
voice … He
excoriated the
Jews and the
socialists, and
promised lower
taxes, higher
wages, more jobs,
better housing and
cheaper fertilizer
… not just assent
[from the crowd]
but ecstasy."

1932

Unemployment

reaches a
staggering six
million, out of a
population of 67
million.

24 Dr Ko lights butter lamps
Monastery, north-eastern Tibet, 1932

Shadows swirl in dark cave of *Gompa*.
We chant mantras, *malas* click, click, click.
Pray to Buddhas. I light butter lamps for Felix –

Om Mani Peme Hung. Om Mani Peme Hung.

watch small flames flick, chase darkness
in arcs. May his life be long, may his work
prosper. He is not Buddha yet, but his desire

Om Mani Peme Hung. Om Mani Peme Hung.

to help beings is true. He is never far from
my prayers. I call upon *Sanjai Manla* – Medicine
Buddha – to bless his work. Far apart in miles

Om Mani Peme Hung. Om Mani Peme Hung.

but hearts and purpose joined. Let him be
showered with auspicious circumstances.
May his hands not err, bring relief to many.

25 A cartolina from Felix
Berlin, 1932

Dear Ciano,

Just a brief note to let you know your pestering
has paid off and I have decided to add Rome to
my yearly European circuit from May. Elisabeth
will accompany me and handle the bookings.

Perhaps you and the Contessa would care to join me
for supper on the 18th? I will still have rooms at the
Excelsior while they make the necessary alterations to
the apartment.

Il tuo,
Felix

Hitler uses
a mixture of
political acuity,
cunning and
deception in
planning the many
steps necessary
to achieve
his goals. He
publicly disavows
violence, and
says he plans
to gain power
by democratic
means, but
intends to
establish a
dictatorship
so that he can
institute the
Nazi agenda.
He intends to
immediately
re-arm Germany,
then occupy
and Germanise
territory to the
East.

26 Felix has lunch with Mussolini: a rhapsody in four courses

Rome, Italy, 1933

I should have tales about the politics we speak,
recount how the Great Man sees Fascism's

future in the world but instead I recall how,
at blade's first contact, the spatchcock

melts from the bone! How sublime the pasta –
tagliatelle con sugo di porcini e crema. I have

to taste that fabulous infusion again (merest
hint of tarragon?). Benito is launched on a

favourite theme – how hard the Germans are,
their total lack of gaiety or humour, essentially

barbarians still. Between mouthfuls I nod accord.
I hope he does not think me rude for interrupting,

asking if the palazzo chef might furnish me with
the recipe – I am desperate to add it to my files.

Then *filetto*, processionally from the kitchen.
Maître d' at the head, cloched silver salver aloft,

junior waiters in train with vegetables (austerity
be damned – six separate covered platters!).

At the rear the largest silver gravy boat I have
ever seen. It is performance, as only Italians do,

theatre for an audience of two – Il Duce and me.
The beef in all its glory is revealed, monarch

of the meal. A flourish and neat bow by the Maître.
He carves succulent slices for our plates.

The fineness of the meat almost finishes me.
I could drown in the delicious delicacy of the jus –

butter, wine, the juices caramelised, with perhaps
a touch of stock. Semifreddo for dessert –

creamy confection to roll around the tongue, relish
the welcome bite of raspberry. To cut the cream.

27 A cartolina from Felix
Rome, 1933

Cara,

Three months seems a very long time. But I will
return on the 15th to treat the King. Will you come
direct to my hotel (I take a suite at The Grand) and
join me for supper?

L'amore da Flick

28 Dr Ko practises life liberation

A monastery, north-eastern Tibet, 1933

I never know exactly how Felix uses massage.
But always plenty chances for *Bodhicitta* –
beings always need relief from pain. I rein in

curiosity, let go attachment to knowing what he
does. Remote here, but travellers bring news.
I hear things not good in host country,

Germany. I go on pilgrimage, this one is last
I think. Three days hike to Moslem slaughter-
yards. Trembling bodies, heaving flanks,

smell of death, fear in creatures' eyes. I buy
freedom for yak. Our scripture say priceless gifts.
For animals – reprieve from being killed, release

from captivity. Gifts for me too – animals' terror
reminds me of good fortune to have human birth,
strengthens determination to prepare for death.

But I want merit to go to Felix, his work be
blessed, so I liberate yak in his name. Verses
of repentance, prayers for threefold refuge.

Om Mani Peme Hung. Om Mani Peme Hung.
Om Mani Peme Hung. Om Mani Peme Hung.
Om Mani Peme Hung. Om Mani Peme Hung.

SA and SS agents (under Himmler) go door-to-door looking for political 'enemies'. Socialists, Communists, trade-union leaders and others who speak out against the regime are arrested and sometimes killed. Their methods are publicised in Nazi-controlled media to increase public fear, docility, obedience and malleability. The SS and SA quickly build a reputation for ruthlessness and terror.

29 Felix admits to awe
Berlin, January 1933

I have just finished treating clients, and am heading
out to join friends for dinner. Traffic is unaccountably

slow; my regular route cordoned off, forcing me
to detour. The *Strassen* throng with people waving

Nazi flags. Then it dawns – today is the day Herr
Hitler is appointed Chancellor. He has now

achieved what many hoped (and some of us feared)
he would achieve. I pause, mesmerised despite

myself by the spectacle. How the Nazis milk every
event for drama! To counter economic strain, they

create festivity, at times of weakness they show
strength. Even I, immune to most of what passes

for politics, am briefly awed by the stiff-limbed,
goose-stepping ranks. Shadows flicker and dance

on young serious faces. I surprise myself by
momentarily believing in them, tall and proud

as Roman soldiers, torches aloft, charged with purpose
and invincibility, scarlet banners emblazoned

with black swastikas against white, each standard
topped by a lofty golden eagle … What am I thinking?

I pull myself away, unsettled to find myself so taken
in by military might masquerading as theatre.

30 Dr Ko explains sky burial
A monastery, north-eastern, Tibet, 1933

Here I have majesty of solitude, uninterrupted
awareness of the Buddha nature of my own mind.
Great lamas – like my *Rinpoche* – die sitting up,

in wooden meditation box. Conscious, as mind
separates from body, resting in clear light many
hours before physical body begins to decay –

thugdham. I hope I die like that, hidden in
luminous *bardo of dharmata*. For forty-nine days
after my death, monks will light butter lamps

to keep hungry ghosts away. Then, lama performs
phowa prayers for my transition. Body will be taken
to consecrated land, open to clear-air-sky

for Sky Burial. Ritually dismembered, blood seeps
into earth, feeds underground creatures. Body is
given to bearded vultures – *lamergeyers* – who wait.

CHAPTER II

31 A Postkarte from Felix
Berlin, 1933

Mein lieber,

Danke for your card. I was very glad to hear from
you and look forward to meeting you on Monday for
coffee at Kranzler's as usual.

Mit den besten Wünschen
Felix

27 February 1933

***Reichstagsbrand-
verordnung***

**(Reichstag fire
decree)**

The Reichstag burns
down, and Hitler
blames this on the
Communists. He
uses this to justify
the Emergency
Decree that
abolishes personal,
press, assembly and
property rights.

32 Felix often thinks of Dr Ko

Berlin, 1933

Sometimes
images of his

face float into
my mind –

serene, eyes
deep pools

of compassion,
ready to crinkle

in wry amusement
at the absurdity

of our human
predicament.

Fierce when
occasion

demanded but
no pettiness

or malice in
the man. I am

yet to meet
his equal.

33 Felix grieves Dr Ko
Berlin, 1933

I do not know
when he will die,

or how, only that
he returns to Tibet

eager to prepare
himself meditatively.

I like to imagine
him sitting in his

meditation box,
his mind as clear

as the mountain air
he so loved. I like

to imagine death
coming to rest a

gentle hand on his
shoulder, coming

to him as friend.
Rest in peace, Dr Ko.

Words from the
Nazi lexicon

**Strafexpedition
(Punitive
Expedition)**

Nazi vigilance
against
Communists
includes "forcing
victims to run a
gauntlet on an
oiled surface
while being
beaten by rubber
clubs".

Dachau,
Germany,
March 1933

**Konzentrations-
lager or KZ
(Concentration
camp)**

The first Nazi
concentration
camp opens
at Dachau
to hold and
torture political
opponents and
union organisers.
Himmler is put
in charge of this
bourgeoning
portfolio.

34 The librarian witnesses the burning
Berlin, 10 May 1933

*"Dort, wo man Bücher verbrennt, verbrennt man auch am Ende
Menschen"* (Where they burn books, they will also ultimately
burn people). – German Jewish poet Heinrich Heine, 1820–21

The room offers sanctuary, holding her while adrenaline
palsies her limbs. At the back of her eyes flames flare.

Singed skin, the reek of burning, as if bodily doused.
Images repeat – spiralling smoke, black and acrid,

soldiers' mouths pulled out of shape, their arms arcing
to lob handfuls of hate. Thousands of flimsy pages ascend

on updrafts like souls departing. Her arms reach,
desperate to catch charred paper. Momentary heat,

text lit like a negative, a few seconds straining to decipher
the script before pages collapse to dust in her hand.

*

All day charred odour clings to hair, clothes. All day
griefs gather, tugging hem, hand. All day – the relentless

rain of once-were-words, falling like black snow.
The city's loss reverberates, a dirge repeated.

A city without a library, a library without books? And
she – guardian. So visceral the memories – thick pages,

the must of old volumes. She grieves for the sheer
physicality of books – bodies you can hold in your hand.

Mourns the loss of the sparks within – tolerance,
peace between people, ideas worth killing for.

*

A blanketing dark falls at last. She collapses, drifts, dreams
she is peering through the window. Wind stirs ash into

billows; beauty in the sweep and stoop of floating cinders.
She watches, incredulous. Ideas rise from the ruins,

liberated from the bodies of books, the chastity of words.
Released from the confinement of shelves, stacks, at large

in the world. People rush into the street with faces
upturned. Some who have never known ideas reach and

stretch, feel their touch. Others come running to find
renewal in words. A democracy of words, for all to read.

Words from the
Nazi lexicon,
Berlin, 10 May
1933

**Bücher-
verbrennung
(Book Burning)**

"On a swastika-
bedecked rostrum,
on the Unter den
Linden, a wide
tree-lined street
running past the
University and
the State Opera
House, Goebbels
proclaims:
*The age of
extreme Jewish
intellectualism
has now ended.*"
The book he then
threw on the fire
was the first of
thousands. As
each name was
mentioned "the
crowd booed and
hissed".

35 Felix notices ugliness
Berlin, 1933

I let most of politics wash
over me but yesterday I see

a sign urging a boycott of
Jewish-owned shops. A cold

premonition slips up my
coat-sleeves, under my hem,

momentarily riffling my
usually solid composure.

When did we – the cultured,
the tolerant – become so hateful?

36 Himmler justifies the Blood Purge
Berlin, 30 June 1934

"… we did not hesitate to do
the duty laid down for us

and put guilty friends up against
the wall and shoot them …

we did not talk about it among
ourselves … Each of us found

it appalling yet we are all sure
that if such orders were

necessary again, we would
carry them out as we did then."

Words from the
Nazi lexicon

**_Lebensunwertes
Leben_ (Life
unworthy of life)**

July 1933:
*"The Law for the
Prevention of
Offspring
with Hereditary
Diseases* provides
for the sterilisation
of 'unfit' parents
and potential
parents, as well as
'euthanasia' of the
'defective' and of
'useless eaters'."
The American
Eugenics Society
endorses the law.

Berlin, 26 April
1933

The **Gestapo** is
formed, the name
derived from
Geheime Staats-
polizei.

14 July 1933

The Nazi Party
declares itself the
only political
party in Germany.

Germany, 30
June 1934

***Nacht der langen
Messer* (Night of
the Long Knives)**

After succumbing
to pressure from
others in the
party, Hitler
orders Himmler
to organise the
ambush and
execution of Ernst
Röhm, the SA
General, and his
most important
officers.
Himmler and
the SS become
the most feared
organisation in
Nazi Germany.

37 Felix explains how he works
Berlin, 1934

Nine years since Dr Ko packed his
bags – how very much I owe

to him. Admittedly a fine masseur
when I first meet him – by Western

standards, that is. Learning his style
of Eastern, deep, neural massage

has made my treatments far superior
to others. Now my clinics thrive.

Demanding work, of hands as well
as mind. Sickness confines patients

to punishment cells. To heal, I must
enter those rooms, get to know from

the inside which restraints are used.
Each treatment exhausts me. I only

work with forty clients a year, as every
patient needs multiple sessions over

six to eight weeks. I require total rest
one week in eight. People clamour,

plead – but Elisabeth is a champion
of the firm *no*. She guards my health.

38 Himmler describes the Cathedral of Light

Sixth Party Congress, Nuremberg, September 1934

I am astounded at the impact of those
152 vertical light-beams rising pale

like marble pillars into the night sky,
a monumental building, constructed

before our very eyes. None of the magic is
lost on me, despite knowing in advance.

When those searchlights are switched
on they light me up inside, as well as

the Nürnberger dark. Out of the insubstantiality
of only-light, Hitler's magnificent vision,

his *Tausendjähriges Reich*, is made real
and grand before us. Magnificent, as he is.

Rapture infuses the faces of the Volk, primal
oohs and aahs of wonder and exaltation

from the 700,000 throats, entranced one
and all. They are simple, the Volk, they need

basic pictures painted for them, a future
made visible. It might be Speer who designs

such grandeur but, I reassure myself, he is
a mere tool Hitler uses to dress his dreams.

September 1934

Reichsparteitag **(National Congress of the Party; Nuremberg Rally)**

"[Hitler's] … virtuoso use of lighting / is no different from / his virtuoso use of the truncheon."
– Bertolt Brecht.

Some 10,000 people gather outside Hitler's hotel, shouting: "We want our Führer!" When Hitler finally appears on the balcony they "look up at him as if he was a Messiah, their faces transformed into something positively inhuman … every word … like an inspired word from on high. [Their] critical faculty is swept away … and every lie pronounced is accepted as high truth itself."

39 Felix talks about *Zufriedenheit*
Scheveningen, Nederland, 1935

I am the luckiest of men with everything
a man could wish for – apartments

in Den Haag and Berlin, my estate
at Hartzwalde, quality vehicles. I work

hard then enjoy my rest. I have excellent
companionship, rub shoulders with royalty

and Europe's elite. I am well served by
my staff. But sometimes, at the end

of a peaceful *Wochenende* at the estate,
or on return from travel, I am restless

and cannot find repose. Elisabeth says
she knows how to cure what ails me –

time, she says, to find a special Fraülein
and settle down. Perhaps she is right.

40 Felix's patient gives a testimonial
Berlin, 1935

My doctors give up on me; no treatment works
and they advise a quiet life. But a friend mentions

Dr Kersten's special massage and I consult him,
full fee-paying, like everybody else. Apparently

he treats only those capable of a total cure.
He takes me on, gives me hope, says I will

resume an active life. I make steady progress
when dear Rudi, manager for twenty years, is fired!

They say it's the expense, but I think it is anti-
Semitism – he is the only supervisor they sack.

Bigotry abounds in these awful blighted days.
The Nazis hate us, want to grind us underfoot!

Decree after decree about work, school, where
we can go, what we can do. Holding gravest fears,

we know we have to get away. Luckily we have
savings, not destitute like others. I could not continue

treatment if not for Dr K's generosity. Not strong
enough to travel yet but our aim is emigration.

Ever-gallant Dr K assures me his many wealthy
patients underwrite those in need, like us.

1 April 1935

The Jehovah's
Witnesses
are banned
throughout
Germany as they
refuse to swear
allegiance to the
Nazi state and to
Hitler as leader.

41 Himmler gloats
Berlin, 10 February 1938

Today the Reichstag passed
the *Gestapo Law*. Now we

have the means we have long
sought to patrol the populace,

protect the Führer and eliminate
those inimical to his great work.

We have deprived the scum
of redress, the vermin of means

of appeal – but tell me, where
on earth is the harm in that?

42 Felix talks about meeting Irmgard
Berlin, February 1938

Like all my best memories, dear Irm will in my mind
forever be linked with food – and via food to dearest

Mutti. *Rassolnik* links them – barley soup and dill pickles
cooked in richest chicken stock. My childhood favourite

– I could not get enough of its comfort, its delicious
taste. The night I meet my will-be wife, our hostess

has, unbeknownst to me, searched out an old recipe
for my childhood treat. I know there is a very pretty

Fraülein across the table (my radar, I admit, is honed
to that frequency!) but I cannot give her a single scrap

of notice until I put that final spoonful in my mouth.
I replace my napkin in a swoon of gratitude and joy.

As soon as I can take her in I know she is the girl
for me – we will wed! I tell her but she just laughs –

such a happy sound, her laugh. We correspond for two
months, and then we marry, just as I knew we would.

Words from the
Nazi lexicon,
Berlin, 1930s

*Juden nicht
erlaubt!* (Jews
not allowed!);
*Kauft nicht bei
Juden!* (Do not
buy from Jews!);
*Die Juden sind
unser Unglück!*
(The Jews are
our misfortune!);
*Geh nach
Palästina!* (Go to
Palestine!)

The SA plaster
such signs
outside shops
and restaurants,
in German towns
and villages.
In the USA a
popular radio
program which
draws an audience
of tens of millions,
also includes calls
for a boycott of
Jewish businesses.

43 Elisabeth Lüben talks about Irmgard
Felix's Wilmersdorf apartment, Berlin, 1938

I am present the night he meets her – charming, gay
    Irmgard. He proposes in front
    of us all! She laughs to hear him ask,
    but does not turn him down.
    Just a few months later they wed.
    She is the perfect girl
    for him; pretty, accomplished hostess,
    excellent horsewoman –
    things for which I have no gift.

For me – running his away-from-Hartzwalde social life
    and massage practice. Best of all
    the friendship we share.
    He would never wish to burden Irm
    but he confides in me,
    values my advice.

Who is to say which of us has the better deal?

44 Felix talks about his philosophy
Felix's apartment, Wilmersdorf, Berlin, late 1930s

Berlin, 17 June
1936

Hitler appoints
Heinrich
Himmler Chief
of German
Police.

There is little point in worrying
about what you cannot control –

that has long been my view;
it suits my temperament. Dr Ko

encouraged equanimity, the focus
my work demands helps to discipline

wayward thoughts and worry.
Many of my patients talk about

political fears, about Herr Hitler
raking hatred. I do not like the man

but there is nothing I can do
one way or the other. It will pass,

I tell them. We need to focus
on work, our loved ones, that which

brings us pleasure, and be willing
to lend a helpful hand. All the rest,

I say, will be blown far away by
the always-reliable winds of history.

Berlin,
Germany,
August 1936

In 1931 Germany
is awarded the
1936 Olympic
Games. Goebbels
convinces Hitler
of the propaganda
possibilities
of hosting the
Games. The
banning of Jewish
and Romany
athletes creates
international
controversy
and in response
to threatened
boycotts, the
Germans include
one token part-
Jewish athlete.
Many Jewish
international
athletes resign
from their teams.
All signs bearing
the words *No
Jews*, or *Jews Not
Welcome Here*
are removed for
the duration of
the games and
replaced after they
conclude.

45 Irmgard talks about the matrimonial bed
Den Haag, Nederland, 1938

Felix had the suite specially made and made to last.
My first glimpse is my wedding night. Famous turner
for the carved and fretted headboard, wash-stand,
dressing table with a small stool to match. Solid,
reassuring pieces, transforming room to refuge.

An honest wood – dark with deeper reddish tones
where light catches it after polish. I often take a cloth
myself, elbow-grease a shine. French bed and table
linen, thick with delicate lace trim. Quality-ware,
monogrammed *K*. Personal wedding gift from he to me.

46 Felix talks about his Heartworld
Gut Hartzwalde, 1938

I buy the land in '31 from a windfall, build the house,
have furniture specially made, purchase Flemish art.

Later I acquire adjoining land, enlarge the house,
clear and beautify the grounds, put acres under crops.

I construct workshops, a dairy – accoutrements
of a substantial, working estate. Irm and I are building

up a stable of thoroughbreds, herds of cattle, farmyard
animals. My aim is self-sufficiency. At first I think

retirement, but war looms – shortages will occur –
the more we grow the better off we will be. By '37

when I marry Irm, the place is doing well. Productive, ja,
but tranquillity is what I cherish most; ambling down

the lane under the arms of ancient oak, riding my cart
with the clop-clop of horseshoe accompaniment. I take

my favourite forest paths, loiter by the running streams.
Idyllic retreat, protected from the strife of life. We still

live at Scheveningen in Den Haag, pleasant house
and gardens, all the cosmopolitan advantages. But

Hartzwalde snares our hearts. We holiday here
at every chance. Irm loves it as much as I. She is a fine

horsewoman, excellent manager of flocks and herds.
It is here I help her birth our first child, a son, Ulf, in '38.

Words from the
Nazi lexicon,
Austria,
March 1938

**Anschluss
(Union)**

The Nazis have
developed their
skill in using
language to
manipulate and
obscure reality.
The invasion
and forcible
annexation of
Austria becomes
a 'union', and (in
a terrible irony)
the language
of 'rights' and
protection is used
as an excuse
to invade other
countries. The
Anschluss is
among Hitler's
first major steps
to create
his thousand-year
Reich.

47 Irmgard talks about becoming a mother
Gut Hartzwalde, 1938

Felix arranges his appointments so he can spend
the final weeks of my confinement at Hartzwalde.
We miss him when he is not here, so much of his
time spent abroad. He wants to aid in my delivery –
the first. Oh, I know he has studied; he reminds me

how many animals he has midwifed. But *really*,
animals are one thing, human beings another! …
In the end he does a good job, calming me, helping me
ease into labour's rhythm, anchored by his strong, safe
hands. A son! Sturdy, contented like his father.

48 A word from Irmgard's lexicon
Gut Hartzwalde, 1938

***Gemütlichkeit* (Cosiness, genial togetherness)**

Evening has fallen, drapes are drawn; the draft
is stoppered at the door. No engagements
take Felix out into the chill. The meal is
cleared away, hot *Kakao* on the silver
salver given by a patient. He is busy

with papers, I have accounts to settle, Ulf
is safe in his crib. No need for words. Not only
cosiness but belonging permeates – armchairs
close to the hearth, stretched and stockinged
feet. Beyond this room, a wild and wicked world.

49 Kristallnacht: the lead-up
Berlin, late 1938

They say it is spontaneous; an unsolicited eruption of
the feeling of the Volk. But Hitler spends eight

years slipping scraps to the dog under the table. Anti-
semitism is the dog he feeds, fattens, leashed until

he is ready for it. Beginning almost immediately –
bans on kosher butchering, boycotts of Jewish

businesses, bans on any Jews owning firearms.
The *Völkischer Beobachter* reads: "Jews For Sale,

Who Wants Them?" Morsels for the rabid dog.
Not too much too soon, whittling away Jewish rights,

citizenship, land, respect. By '38 the dog is slavering,
straining at the leash. All he has to do is slip the clasp.

50 Kristallnacht: the facts
Berlin, 27 October 1938

Bigger, bolder Hitler boots 12,000 Polish Jews
living on German soil back to Poland.

Zindel Grynszpan is one. Hanoverian since 1911,
children, his own tailor shop. The Nazis plunder

everything – property, possessions, place in the
world. Trains from all over Germany arrive near

the border. The SS order the 12,000 to walk
to a transit camp. Those who cannot "are beaten

until the road is red with their blood". Stranded,
forgotten – without the Red Cross they will starve.

Decades-long German residents, they are friends,
community members, they pay German taxes –

in the Nazi scheme, all of it means zilch. Zindel's
17-year-old son Herschel, a Parisian rabbinical

student, buys a 6.35-calibre gun from a shop called
The Sharp Blade, buys 25 bullets, takes the Métro

to the German Embassy. In the name of the 12,000
he fires five metal slugs into the soft, yielding belly

of the Embassy's third secretary – Ernst vom Rath.
Hitler sends his personal physician but vom Rath

dies anyway. Herschel's postcard to his parents reads:
"I must, so the whole world hears my protest."

51 Kristallnacht: slipping the leash
Berlin, late October 1938

Hitler and Minister Goebbels confer,
see propaganda potential too good

to miss. A hook, they think, on which
to hang the blame. "Vom Rath's

assassination," they bluster, "is part
of the Jewish conspiracy for world

domination!" Two weeks later, the glass
begins to break. Long hours of terror

in the night. Brownshirt thugs rampage.
"Pull back the police," Goebbels and Hitler

declare, "the Jews should for once feel
the anger of the people." The Volk's

violence is officially endorsed. Daylight
brings no pause. By the end: hundreds

of synagogues are burnt (fires pierce
the night); hundreds of Jews are killed,

bashed, publicly humiliated; 30,000 Jews
are relocated to concentration camps,

7,500 Jewish businesses are destroyed
(spears and crystals of glass). Overnight

the city has become another city –
with a foretaste of Armageddon.

52 The lone voice of protest
Melbourne, Australia, 1938

Resounding silence inside Germany and out.
No word from neighbours, service clubs,

churches. No government anywhere in the world
utters even token protest. How the Nazi brass

exult to have got away with so much! One lone
voice rings out: 78-year-old Yorta Yorta man,

William Cooper, delivers a petition to the German
Consulate in Melbourne. Permitted through the gate

and up the steps, he is halted there – the Consul
refuses him entry, refuses to come out from behind

his door. From one persecuted people to another,
William Cooper speaks across continents directly

to Herschel Grynszpan and the millions to follow:
"I hear you, I see your suffering, you are not alone."

53 Himmler gushes
Chancellery, 1939

I hope it pleases the Führer
that in just six years the SS

has grown to 240,000 men.
So big now that we have

to organise into divisions.
Our target is always those

who threaten our dear leader
and natürlich the ubiquitous

Untermensch. We must be
ruthless in cleansing the Reich

of such scum. "The best political
weapon is the weapon of terror.

Cruelty commands respect.
Men may hate us. But, we

do not ask for their love; only
for their fear." We publicise

our methods, courtesy of Herr
Goebbels, so the Volk know

we are serious about the task
entrusted to us. The basement

of Prinz-Albrecht-Strasse
and the cleansing that happens

there is rightly the most feared
place in all of Germany.

54 The devoted father

A photo of Himmler with his daughter Gudrun
(Puppi), 1938

Hers is a face innocent of transgression.
You shudder for her future (which already

has been lived, suffering it was hers
to have – already had).The photo is black-

and-white but you know the dress will be
buttercup yellow, heartbreakingly pastel.

You know it can't end well for her and that
her innocence – in the perfectly even

curve of a double peter-pan collar
and the gathered, cuffed sleeves which

puff like a sleeping child's breath, the bow
lying so carefully against her chest, its child

heart tucked safely behind the even yoke
of her dress, its gentle folds sewn by some-

one's painstaking hand, chosen this special
day with care – will be destroyed. Light

blurs her father's spectacles. She sits close
on his lap, he leans against her strength.

55 Herr Diehn recommends a patient
Berlin, 1938

August Diehn at your command, current head
of the Deutsche Kalium Syndikat – our business

Potassium. I have known Felix for many years –
as a patient and a friend. We are close – a favour-

sharing friendship. He has treated me, with
excellent results, and I have done him many

good turns. I recommended August Rosterg
and a host of other industry heads. My referrals

bulk his practice, make him wealthy; now bookings
need be made a month ahead. Things in Deutschland

are looking dire – politically, I mean. The Nazi
star rises and garners real support. Hitler works

himself into a fury and the people love him.
But I despair. I never can interest Felix in politics

though I tell him the Nazis are our enemies,
they will wreck the country. "They are sowing

hatred (I hammer the point home), and hatred
they will reap!" We are desperate – rumours run

they plan to nationalise industry. Socialism
threatens our industry, ja, but more, it will smash

the whole economy. We are keen for debate
but that is unlikely – perhaps leverage instead?

I hear Himmler ails – at times he is prostrate
with pain. If we can get Felix to treat him,

could he persuade Himmler to reconsider,
have him convince Hitler not to go ahead?

56 Irmgard drives Felix to Chancellery
Gestapo Headquarters, Chancellery, 10 March 1939

I cannot pretend I am happy
about Felix's decision, but
I have exerted all the pressure
I am willing to exert. It is his
choice. I am not prepared

to argue his medical ethics –
he refuses no-one – even
Herr Himmler. I drive him
into Berlin, to Chancellery,
the infamous Gestapo
Headquarters where

Himmler has his lair. Felix's
first meeting with the man.
My heart sinks as I watch him
stride up those marble stairs,
his back as straight

as his walking stick, briefcase
tucked under his arm, past
the goose-stepping soldiers,
stiff as statues, between the
huge columns and underneath

the spreadwinged eagle – even
Felix's not inconsiderable size
is dwarfed by such a solid
impenetrable immensity. I
shudder as he enters the place.

Munich, 30 September 1938

***Münchner Abkommen* (The Munich Agreement)**

Nazi Germany gains the so-called 'Sudetenland' by annexing portions of Czechoslovakia. Germany, France, the UK and Italy sign an agreement in Munich to allow Germany to take over this territory, while Czechoslovakia is not invited. This is appeasement, driven by a desire to ensure 'peace in our time', in Neville Chamberlain's words.

23 August
1939

***Molotov-
Ribbentrop-Pakt
(Soviet-German
Non-Aggression
Pact)***

The Nazis and
Soviets agree
not to attack one
another, and add
a secret protocol
that divides
Eastern Europe
between them.

57 Felix realises this is where Dr Ko has brought him

Chancellery, 10 March 1939

The biggest shock is how he looks – I have seen
photographs – I thought I knew what to expect.

But he is weedy, with a narrow chest, weak chin,
and hair as dark as soot. His jaw recedes, shoulders

slope, his paunch pokes above his belt – hardly
an exemplar of the virile man! He goes on about racial

purity but cannot he see that he himself looks Mongolian!
I am businesslike, letting just my skill touch his skin.

He writhes, begs for release. A man like any man
tormented. Pinched is too small a word for the mess

his nerves are in. No energy can pass through that ganglia
of knots and burls. As my fingers bite into him he

moans. Hard work for me, agony for him, but gradually
torque improves, his writhing stops and something

approaching peace softens his face – incredulous
my massage works when so many quacks have failed.

*

Too soon to broach potassium but I figure how it might
be done. Before treatment he is shut inside the locked

and bolted room of pain. His only words are from
the soliloquy of pain. But in the aftermath he opens

up, confides he is a tool for Hitler's will. His whole
demeanour changes, chest puffs out, eyes glaze with

adoration. Maybe his willingness to confide will permit
me to put a case? Perhaps a warning – should they

socialise, they risk huge financial loss. Big backers
would leave in droves. How financially risky this would
be! Behind urbanity he is sticky into power, spins a web.

I need to watch myself, spin my own. Towards the end

my first test comes. "Doktor, in gratitude, immediately
I shall have you enrolled in the SS with the rank

of Colonel!" Me, military, don Nazi garb? Nein danke!
But more to the point – it is not safe to be beholden

to Herr H. Just as well I sharpened my wits to rapiers
before I walked in the Gestapo door. I bow my formal

thanks. "Impossible to accept," I say. "Holland is my
home with house and wife, extensive clientele." But I will

attend him in Berlin when he needs me to still his pain.
I think I get away with it – time will tell. Normally I do not

countenance a case without hope of total cure but this
is Himmler after all – refusing does not seem wise.

Words from the
Nazi lexicon,
31 August 1939

***Operation
Himmler or
Operation
Konserve*
(Operation
Himmler or
Operation
Canned Goods)**

Designed to
create the
appearance of
aggression by
Poland against
Germany to
justify Germany's
attack.

Dressed in
Polish uniforms,
"German troops
storm various
buildings on the
border, scare
the locals with
shots, carry out
vandalism, and
retreat, leaving
behind dead
bodies wearing
Polish uniforms.
The bodies
were actually
prisoners from
concentration
camps; ...
dressed in
Polish uniforms,
killed by a
lethal injection,
then shot for
appearance."

58 Himmler talks about Operation Konserve

Chancellery, 1939

Not only a military Blitzkreig
to reclaim German territories

in the East but Hitler plans
a *propaganda blitzkrieg*

as well. Genius! It will stop
England and France in their

conniving tracks. He entrusts
to me crucial components:

how to make Poland appear
the aggressor, to legitimise

our invasion. I own I have
come up with a brilliant

scheme of *Schall und Rauch*,
magicians' smoke and mirrors.

Greatly relieved to find myself
equal to the occasion, the calibre

of the Führer and his vision. They
will be eating from our hands.

59 Felix contemplates Himmler
Chancellery, 1939

On my second visit I have time to take in more
of my surrounds. There are guards with machine

guns everywhere. People; uniformed, stiff, correct,
and busy. I appear to be the only civilian amongst

a sea of soldiers. They practise the ridiculous
outstretched arm Nazi salute and Prussian clicking

heels at every chance. Guards take me up one cold,
marble staircase after another – I hear Chancellery

used to be a museum, bizarre provenance for Nazi
HQ. H's Secretary, Dr Brandt, greets me in the ante-

room, shows me where to hang my coat and hat,
lean my cane. Himmler is engaged, he says pleasantly,

will be with me shortly. He attends his work while
I am happy to wait, pondering the strange twist

of fate which brings me here. I think back to the first
session, the dreadful state of H's sympathetic nerve,

impossibility of a total cure. He tried to induct me
as a Nazi! I sense steel behind his manners.

My work will be cut out for me, not only in delivery
of effective treatment but in dealing with the man.

Poland,
1 September 1939

The Battle and Surrender of Warsaw

After a huge 26-day aerial bombardment by the Luftwaffe and attacks by the German army, Warsaw surrenders on 27 September; 140,000 Polish troops are taken prisoner by the German invaders. "The smell lingers for weeks: charred plaster, burning oil and cordite."

3 September 1939

Declaration of War on Germany by France and the United Kingdom.

60 Felix is shocked
Berlin, 1939

I am out driving with the Herr today
when he shows another aspect of his

multi-faceted, strange personality.
In a car next to ours, driven by their

parents, are two blond, blue-eyed
children. I am amazed when he tells

his driver to stop them. He rushes
to the back door, and under the wide-eyed

stares of their parents, takes one boy
in his arms, almost drooling over him.

Pale with emotion, he is overcome
by his encounter with these exemplars

of the superior Aryan race! The parents
dart looks at each other, unnerved

by his emotion, unsure whether to be proud
or terrified to have individual attention

from the Reichsführer. He takes both
children's names and addresses so he

can send gifts. He turns to me, the light
of twisted romantic obsession making

his eyes shine, his normally nondescript
face lit up and says: "Look, Herr Kersten –

this is what all our people should look
like. One day I'll have him for our SS."

61 Felix learns about the levers
Chancellery, 1939

Such an enigma! Once his knots have unravelled,
his nerve unwinds, then his tongue undergoes a similar

liberation. He talks non-stop, astounds me by confiding
fears of cancer – dreads dying as his father did.

He seems to trust me … in repose, rescued from
the pincer grip of pain, he admits to shame of his illness,

how he hides his sweats, nausea, cramps. He lives
in fear any in his entourage will discover his secret vice –

sickness! I remonstrate that illness deserves compassion,
makes us human. Not for the Reichsführer! I may as well

address my words to the wall. I risk censure or worse
for expressing such un-Nazi thoughts. My first test

was declining the uniform, the offer of SS captaincy.
My next is arguing against him. Will he call the guards?

When he broaches the socialist agenda I raise the fears
of industry as put by my potassium friends. He tells me

it is old news – the Nazis have abandoned the socialist
part of their platform for now. At least he does not call

for my arrest. I know I am pushing boundaries that I
do not imagine many do. But maintaining independence

is crucial – I am not the sort to be obsequious but –
is it possible with Reichsführer Himmler?

Words from the
Nazi lexicon,
Poland, 8
October 1939

Ghetto **(Ghetto)**
The first ghetto for
Jews established
by the Nazis
is located
at Piotrków
Trybunalski,
38 days after
the invasion of
Poland.

Words from the
Nazi lexicon,
Germany,
October 1939

***Gnadentod*
(Mercy death)**

The euphemism
given to the Nazi
forced euthanasia
program. Doctors
are directed to
judge certain
patients including
those with
intellectual,
physical and
psychiatric
disabilities
as 'incurably
sick' and then
administer 'mercy
death'. Aktion
T4 is the postwar
designation for
this program.

At least 70,273
people are
killed at various
extermination
centres located
at psychiatric
hospitals in
Germany and
Austria.

62 Himmler pontificates on hunting
Chancellery, 1939

"Poor creatures browsing on the edge
of the wood, innocent, defenceless,

unsuspecting. Properly considered
it's pure murder. I've often bagged

a deer but I must tell you I have had
a bad conscience each time I've looked

into its dead eyes … No, Herr Kersten,
don't talk to me about hunting.

I don't care for so crude a sport.
Nature is so marvellously beautiful.

Every animal has the right to live.
Buddhist monks, when they pass

through a wood in the evening,
carry a bell with them, to make

any woodland animal keep away,
so that no harm will come to them."

63 Himmler's agonia
Gestapo Headquarters, Berlin, 1939

Pain dogs me down the years
past my best defences, drives

me to the pain room, bolts
the door. Pain takes off gloves,

unsheathes a sharpened claw.
When pain has finished, shame

takes its place with whip and
spur. Dare call yourself Reichsführer

SS! You cringing dog, what kind
of human lump are you?

Words from the
Nazi lexicon

**Einsatzgruppen
(Task forces)**

Death squads
made up mainly
of SS and police
personnel, formed
under Himmler's
direction and
operating in
German-occupied
territories after the
invasion of Poland
in 1939. They
are given the task
of mass killings,
principally by
shooting, mostly
of civilians.

64 Felix at table with the Himmlers
Gmund am Tegernsee, Germany, 1939

At least my belly growls no protest. Casseroles
and soups, fruit after meals, home-baked *Kuchen*

morning and afternoon. Simple country fare,
but plenty of it … Brandt phoned me in Den Haag.

Not asked or requested but summoned me. "He is ill
at Gmund," curt, clipped, "in agony, wants you there

post-haste. Close to München, on Lake Tegernsee.
The auto will collect you from the station. Already

the rooms I have booked for you at the inn. All your
meals you will be taking with them." I go. He keeps

a modest house, never takes more than his fair share.
The setting is sublime – lake, forest, birds. His wife

Marga, children – Gudrun, and an adopted boy.
At table he likes to play mine host. His geniality

is a shock. The children eat with us, are excused H's
postprandial lectures. Pet themes predominate –

the charms of his native Bavaria, time past when
it ruled itself; the lessons, courtesy Schoolmaster H,

which history tells. He particularly relishes tales
of William the Fowler, hero-worships him, imagines

himself a modern reincarnation. Repeatedly I bite
my tongue, accept another homegrown plum.

*

When I first arrive he is close to passing out but keeps
to rigid manners. Cold skin, wet with the effort not

to hunch, not to stoop. He will not bend before we step
behind closed doors. I set to work. I delve, he writhes.

He pants, bites his bottom lip, clenches blankets
in desperate, clammy hands. His pain peaks, he pales.

Slowly the nerve responds, colour ventures back.
We talk between the work. "The Führer longs for war,"

he declares that first day, "no peace until the world is
purified by war." A crazy litany, from Hitler verbatim,

never questioned. He stares away, imagining
the *Tausendjähriges Reich*? No surprise after Prague,

it is all they talk of in Den Haag. I risk seeming weak or
worse. "But war will bring Europe to her knees," I argue.

He argues back, vehement, but does not call the Gestapo
to snuff me out. I return gratefully to my hotel, relieved

I did not succumb to silence. Blessed liberty until
the evening meal. The woods around the lake are balm.

I walk their paths, turning his words, the Führer's,
and the terrifying prospect of war, over in my mind.

65 Felix talks about Russia invading Finland

Felix's apartment, Wilmersdorf, Berlin, 1939

I may not have been born
there but Finland has been

good to me and it grieves me
that the country of my birth

has invaded my adopted
country. The least I can do

is return assistance when
she is in need. I have started

a collection. I have raised
guilders from the Netherlands,

secured furs from England,
medicines and ambulances

from France, and from Italy
arms and aircraft. But that

pact Hitler signed with Stalin
in '39 makes everyone here

reticent about sticking their
neck out to help Finns.

66 Felix asks: are we safe at Scheveningen?
Nederland, April 1940

Amidst all the fear and broken
glass of occupation, at least they

manage their escape – our Queen
and her Prince – all the way

to England. Last month Norway
keeled, Denmark, Belgium will

be next. All over Holland the streets
are silent with the Kinder gone.

The Government has fallen,
they have put Nazis in their place.

Jewish shops are shut and shuttered
until pure Aryans can be found.

Many of my friends hide. We are
heartsore for the loss of life,

for the strife that happens all
around. Irm and I are safe here

in our home, for now. Himmler
has been my patient since March,

already he leans on me. He knows
I pose no threat, being firmly

of a politically neutral cast. In
any case he relies on me. I hope

I am not wrong in thinking I can
count on him for our protection.

CHAPTER III

67 Felix and Irmgard are forced to move
to Gut Hartzwalde

Scheveningen, Nederland, April 1940

Yes, I feel safe in Holland, even though Europe
is coming apart at the seams. But that does

not stop them coming for me. The crunch
of tyre-tread announces them – Himmler's SS

barrelling down my drive! Arriving on his
orders; they sneer, delight in threatening

us, seeing me ill at ease in front of Irm.
The Gestapo decides all foreigners must

leave or else accept surveillance. I threaten
to appeal to my embassy – they laugh,

tell me the Finns will not declare war with
Germany over me! Then they deliver

the coup de grâce – we are to be interned
at Hartzwalde! Not only does H fail to protect

us, he orders this to happen! I talk it over
with Irm – we know we have no choice,

agree to comply. H is positioning me
to be his personal physician, always close

at hand. All right, but I think I have more sway
than this. I return to Berlin and turn my anger

and incomprehension on him. He says:
"My dear Doktor Kersten, you have to realise

that I only want to save our sister country,
that purely Germanic country, from

the capitalist Jews that have enslaved her."
There is no arguing with his madness. He

sincerely believes that dear Queen Wilhelmina,
her family and Ministers are Jewish spies!

68 Irmgard talks about leaving Den Haag
Gut Hartzwalde, April 1940

So quiet here after the bustle of Den Haag.
As soon as the cases are unpacked I go
to the stables and greet my best chestnut.
I have him saddled and before the day is out
have taken a grand reconnaissance ride,

fence to fence. After so many idle months,
it does not take long to find my seat,
the horse his stride. The best thing about living
here full-time – I can ride every day, a free hand
to build up the stables and our breeding line.

69 Felix feels his fetters
Gut Hartzewalde, 1940

We are only forty miles from Berlin and
Herr Himmler has me where he wants me.

Not only does he want me on hand for
himself but he loans me out to others

in his entourage, as if I am a piece of sporting
equipment to be shared around … fascinating

glimpse into the men who hold the Nazi
reins of power. For all their talk of Aryan

perfection, they are an unhealthy lot – stomach
cramps their complaint du jour. In January

Foreign Minister Ribbentrop does not endear
himself to me – ignorant, foolish man, who

will not even stir himself to remember my name.
Now H has me treating the Head of the German

Labour Front, Robert Ley. *Reichstrunkenbold*,
they call him, resident Reich drunkard.

Often obnoxious, always drunk. Soon I will
treat his wife whom he mistreats appallingly.

What worries me is how to keep confidentiality –
I know H assumes I will pass on knowledge

of his peers so he can garner extra purchase
in this the lethal game of politics they play.

70 Felix explains a word from his lexicon
Berlin, 1940

***Muckefuck* (Ersatz coffee)**

Today, not able to procure a cup of real Kaffee
anywhere, I had my first mouthful of the impostor

which masquerades as coffee in these dire
Blockaded days. If it had not been impolite,

if I had been in the privacy of my own rooms,
I would have spat it out in disgust. It tastes just

as you would expect with a name like that.
Fig, acorn, malt, barley, chicory and dandelion –

admire their ingenuity, but taste? Mein Gott!
Taste it has not. More like a mouthful of brackish

dishwater. I will do many things for the war effort
but drink this rubbish? I think not!

71 Felix visits the Finnish Ambassador
Berlin, 1940

I do not know where to turn. Himmler is dragging me
into his lair and I am powerless. Heady at first to be

so close to the source of power, but will I burn? Both
Irm and Elisabeth hate me treating H – they know

I have little choice but are vehement. As a Finnish citizen
I pay Kivimäki, Finnish Ambassador in Berlin, a discreet

visit. His anti-Nazism is well known – I expect him to tell
me to get the hell out of Himmler's web, but he sits up

straight at his desk, leans towards me, insists I have a duty.
"You must continue to treat Himmler," he says, "glean

every intelligence and perhaps you'll find a way to help
our Nationals." Kivimäki does not give me a choice, sees

a possibility I have not conceived. "And besides," he says,
"should you leave, it could turn Himmler against Finland.

No, man, you have to stay. Make sure you report to us."
I enter the Legation seeking help to leave the country

and the snare I find restraining me. I leave down-
cast with the teeth of another fetter biting tight.

Words from the
Nazi lexicon,
Poland, 1940

***AB-Aktion,
Ausserordentliche
Befriedungsaktion***
**(Extraordinary
Pacification
Action)**
A benign-sounding,
systematic program
of terror, murder
and cruelty,
executing members
of Poland's middle
and upper classes:
doctors, teachers,
priests, landowners,
and businessmen
are rounded up and
killed. More than
30,000 Poles are
arrested and 7,000
Polish leaders are
massacred.

72 Felix aboard Himmler's rolling HQ
Sonderzug Heinrich, somewhere in German-occupied Europe, May 1940

"Pack your bags, my dear Doktor," is what he said,
"we're leaving tomorrow for the front!" He offered

it as if a gift – certainly not imagining I might wish
to decline. Clearly I have no choice – he wants me

on hand, in case. I have a private compartment
and porter – a good-natured, devoted family man,

secretly not interested in National Socialism.
Meals in the communal dining car with H's officers

– more raucous and arrogant by the day. All services
under his command are here – Gestapo, SS,

Intelligence and Counter-Intelligence, personnel
in control of occupied territories. Totally surrounded

by Nazis of every hue – some who want my neck.
Only H's known patronage lets me keep my skin.

He buoys his troops with hope, congratulates
their many successes, steels their determination,

plans the next stages of the war. But it revolts me
and I hardly maintain the rudiments of strained civility.

73 Felix writes a journal entry
Sonderzug Heinrich, somewhere in German-occupied
Europe, May 1940

My days are so filled with tedium that I have
decided to keep a journal. I will have my secretary,

Frau Wacker, type it up on my return. Excellent
insurance. I treat H between 1000 and 1100 hours

each morning, our conversations the only real break
in my isolation. Fascinating windows into how

the man thinks, his multiple prejudices. Today
we returned to arguing anti-Semitism. I reiterate

my lack of comprehension, as the Jews contribute
everywhere they live. Of course each race has

exceptions – the lazy, the immoral. But to judge
and reject a whole race – it makes no sense!

H argues with his customary blinkered vehemence –
another zealot at a time when zealotry abounds.

I let his charged words wash over me, breathe,
take up the reins again, resume his treatment.

Then lunch and I have the rest of the day to fill,
nominally at liberty but it is the strangest kind

of tethered, fearful freedom. I am invited to use H's
library, astounded at his titles: medieval herbalism,

archaeology, astrology and history. Many works
of significant scholarship. Alas, despite the library's

breadth, reading only narrows the man, confirms
him in his many prejudices. The books that claim

my interest are clustered together on the shelves:
Vedas, Bible, Gospels, Koran, treatises on theology,

mystical writings, works on the Church's jurisdiction.
When I query him during a pause, he replies they

are his 'tools of trade', that Hitler has given him
a most important task – to draw up a new Bible

of the German faith. "Once Christianity is crushed,"
he says, face serious, eager, "Hitler will replace

Christ as the saviour of humanity!" I hang my head
so H will not see my appalled incredulity.

74 Felix finds a friend in an unlikely place
Sonderzug Heinrich, somewhere in German-occupied
Europe, May 1940

H asks me to see his Private Secretary, Dr Rudolf
Brandt, who shares the most common Nazi complaint –

stomach pains. At first we circle each other – this train
is a hotbed of distrust and betrayal and only fools

would trust each other too soon. But I treat him
on consecutive days and we get to know each other.

Cautiously his nervous system responds to my work,
recalls what it is to relax and let go. They seem so

strong, but these Nazi bodies suffer the torment
of chronic strain. Brandt works under the most exacting

boss and is up till early morning fulfilling H's demands.
Physically he pays the price. As I get to know his body

I get to know the man. Slowly and subtly with silence
and innuendo more than outright statement we realise

we are of accord. He is idealistic, horrified by how
the leaders comport themselves, disgusted by obvious

corruption. The relief of saying what I truly feel!
He warns me they are at H again, planting and feeding

seeds of distrust of me – I must constantly watch my back.
But amongst the strife, perhaps I have made a friend.

Words from the
Nazi lexicon,
10 May 1940

***Fall Gelb* (Case
Yellow)**

The name of the
German military
plan to invade
Western Europe.
This includes
the invasion
of Holland,
Luxembourg
and Belgium.

15 May 1940

The RAF flies its
first bombing raid
on Germany.

75 Felix contemplates the fall of France
Sonderzug Heinrich, somewhere in German-occupied
Europe, June 1940

I grieve when each European
country succumbs – but I think

the fall of France affects me most.
I hoped that after the first shock

of Nazi tanks rolling down
her boulevards she would shrug

them off like last time, but today,
seeing the gloat on H's weasel

face, hearing the news, I admit
to myself that France too has gone

Germany's way. He invites me to
come with him to Compiègne

to witness Pétain sign the armistice.
Jubilant success for him would be

torture for me. I decline. The world
is in a sad and sorry mess and I am

feeling very low. One by one the
great lights are being extinguished.

76 Irmgard reflects
Gut Hartzwalde, August 1940

H has Flick on a very tight leash; he only has
to tug and Felix is obliged to run. Elisabeth
and I both warned him at the beginning when
he had a choice – but now, well, it would be
suicide to refuse. F has very little left of his liberty

and he chafes against restraint. Returning to
Berlin after weeks at the front, H surprises us
by giving F leave to join Ulf and me at Hartzwalde.
In the last few weeks of pregnancy I am doing
my part for the Vaterland, hoping for another son.

Although perhaps it is dangerous to even think it,
a daughter may be safer in these times of war.
F's father has moved in with us finally at ninety
caring for himself is just too much. Still capable
of a full day's work and he contributes a lot.

All of us love having Flick home. I go into labour
just before he is due back at Chancellery. He is midwife
once again. This time I know the ropes, ease into
labour like an old hand. I have a second son; healthy,
happy. Felix and Ulf both dote; we name him Arno.

Words from
Churchill,
London, 4 June
1940

**"We shall fight
on the beaches"**

Following the
success of
German forces
in Europe and
the evacuation
of the British
Expeditionary
Force from
Dunkirk, Churchill
delivered a
powerful speech
that was designed
to both rouse
and reassure the
British population.
The British would
fight on every
front against Nazi
Germany,
and the Empire
would fight on if
Britain were to
fail.

London, 18 June
1940

**"This was their
finest hour"**

A speech by
Winston Churchill
to the House of
Commons arguing
that if Britain
stood fast it would
go down in history
as Britain's 'finest
hour'.

From July 1940

***Luftschlacht um England* (literally Air battle for England)**

The German airforce (Luftwaffe) campaign against the United Kingdom included extensive bombing raids, during the summer and autumn of 1940.

77 Felix describes the first time he secures a release

Chancellery, 26 August 1940

I actually pull it off! It happens like this: two weeks
ago Rosterg, to whom I owe Hartzwalde, pays me

a visit. Will I intervene for his factory foreman –
a decent, honest man imprisoned in a concentration

camp, for the simple sin of being a Social Democrat.
What can I do? Even the thought of approaching

The Herr with such a request scares me. Rosterg says
he knows I have H's ear – perhaps I can influence him.

It would be absurd, dangerous. I take the details
and promptly forget about them. Two weeks pass

when H calls me for a debilitating attack. Gruelling
work, but one by one, with extreme exertion,

I manage to undo his knots – for now. Because
his gut has been so twisted he is even more grateful

than usual. He says that he feels guilty for never
paying me. Instinctively I know I have an edge –

if I accept money I put myself under his control.
I tell him payment is impossible for incomplete cures.

"And besides," I say, "I know you are of slender means.
It is a principle with me never to accept payment

from poor people, I make rich clients pay for them!"
Never so effusive: "Dear, dear Herr Kersten,

how can I ever thank you?" In a moment of inspiration
I recall Rosterg's request. Pulling the man's details

from my wallet I say: "My fee, Reichsführer – is this
man's freedom!" I see him struggle but in the end

he replies: "As it is you asking, of course I agree."
He calls Brandt to effect the man's release.

Before Brandt leaves the room he locks eyes with me,
seems to offer a wordless glance of support. I file it away

for future reference. Astounded at my leverage,
I leave, buoyed, with adrenaline fizzing in my veins!

78 Felix explains how he becomes
a secret ambassador

Berlin, 1940

In my next meeting with Kivimäki, he tells me
about Bødtker, the Finnish Consul-General

in Oslo – accused of spying for the British.
The Nazis have arrested him. He is imprisoned

and Kivimäki says his life is under serious threat.
Can I help? I am fresh from my success for Rosterg –

perhaps a repeat is possible. I wait until I unknot
H's guts and he is in that post-prandial release

from pain. Always at his most receptive then,
I ask him to consider Bødtker's release as a special

and personal favour to me. While he pauses
to consider, I admit my heart is in my mouth.

Fears rear about the wisdom of taking such a risk,
the danger of my act. I am delivered when he agrees!

Over the next days and weeks I build the number
of cases I put to him. Grown bold, it amazes me

he mostly agrees. I move on to request the release
of many members of the Dutch resistance, Government

leaders, industry heads. They are friends and patients,
I tell him. I cannot always secure their release, often

have to accept H's agreement to commute the death
penalty. Exhausting. Not only the physical demands

of undoing H's knotted nerves, also the pressure
of judging when to bring requests to his attention,

finding the right measure of flattery and bullying
to convince him. I grow skilled at lying and dissembling,

often leave Gestapo HQ on an adrenaline high.
Sometimes it takes the whole evening, with Elisabeth's

help, to come down. When I have had my fill
of the sticky web, the *Wochenende* peace

of Hartzwalde calls – soothing greens and grasses
wash me clean, Irm and boisterous boys are balm.

Utterly spent, but when all around the dark
presses in … at least I know I do some good.

79 Felix acquires an informant
Felix's apartment, Wilmersdorf, Berlin, 1940

Before I leave Holland in the summer I make
arrangements with a friend – I will call him

Mr R – to keep me secretly informed about
affairs there. We develop a code and I give

him my army field address for correspondence.
Together, on this informal footing, we begin

helping our Dutch friends. Not without risk.
One day I arrive to treat H and he is in fine

fettle, almost frothing at the mouth with febrile
accusations about Mr R and I, and the treason

he accuses us of committing. I convince him
of our loyalty, he simmers down. I am growing

adept at 'persuasion', that particularly Nazi skill!
Another day, Rauter, Head of the Gestapo

in Holland, rakes me over the coals, suspicious
about where I get my Dutch data. He seems

more put out that I tell H about arrests before
he has the chance to submit his reports! Despite

their thuggery, appearance of strength – unbending
as tempered steel – they are as insecure as Kinder.

80 Felix sets up his underground
Felix's apartment, Wilmersdorf, Berlin 1940

I need to find a more secure way to
receive information from Mr R.

Back in Berlin I enlist Secretary
Brandt's help. I tell him I have

trouble managing correspondence
from my amorous affairs. He

immediately understands, offers
me use of the Reichsführer's

protected address! Feldpost-
number 35360, to be exact.

I cannot believe such luck
– "the one inviolable number

in Germany," he assures me when
I ask if my letters will really

be safe. H sees me slipping
envelopes into his private satchel.

He smiles in a manly, carnal way,
both envying and taking pity

on my plight. Can it really work?
How extraordinary to be able

to conduct work for the Dutch
underground, under H's very nose!

30 November
1940 and 8
December
1940

**The Rumbula
Massacre (Riga,
Latvia)**

On two
separate days,
Einsatzgruppen
and local
collaborators
massacre 25,000
Jews near the
Rumbula forest.
Apart from
the Babi Yar
massacre in
1941, this
becomes the
biggest two-day
Nazi atrocity.

81 Felix reflects as the year closes
Wilmersdorf, December 1940

Look where my skill has taken me! This second wartime
Yuletide finds me where I never thought to be: rubbing

shoulders with the Nazi elite! Ach, I am used to men
of power – ever since Dr Ko bequeathed me his massage

practice, I have treated Europe's most powerful: royalty,
statesmen, politicians and industrialists. As he said,

underneath our clothes we are all humans. When I first
put my hands on H's body I wondered if it is true for such

a twisted man. He is twisted, no doubt, but massaging
H for a year and a half now, I have proved it: when he gets

knotted up he suffers as any other man. And when I loosen
him, he responds with gratitude and relief. More, amazingly,

I have discovered a way to sway his mind on behalf of
others. A significant chink in the Reichsführer's armour.

I have built on that, set up the rudiments of an underground.
Mr R has fed me data from the ground, and one no less than

the Finnish Ambassador has provided encouragement.
As the year draws to its close, amongst the host

of appalling news there is this small, precious seed
of hope, planted – and growing – amid the Nazi slime.

82 Conte Ciano addresses an assembly
Rome, Italy, 12 December 1940

Benvenuti friends and special guests Dottore e Signora
Felix Kersten from Berlin. His Royal Highness King

Umberto II hosts this gathering to celebrate and award
outstanding service to our country. Dottore Kersten

is this year's recipient. Before we proceed I will share
a small jest with you, per favore. Giving this award

to a mere Dottore is a real aberration. Usually far more
serious enterprises are rewarded than the practice

of Medicine – usually we recognise a person with far
more sophisticated skills, more socially important skills

like the ability to host a lavish dinner – more and more
difficult as shortages worsen! On a more serious note

the award has a notable history. An old order of knight-
hood from 1572, granted by the Royal House of Savoy.

The Order honours distinguished contributors
to la vita italiana. Dottore Kersten is such a man.

Physiotherapist by training, he has developed more than
just manual therapy. He calls it physio-neural massage

and è buono. I know because he treated me and cured
me, as he has cured so many distinguished others,

including members of our own Royal Family. Dottore
Kersten, I hereby award you *La Croce di Commendatore*

dell'Ordine di Lazzaro e Maurizio. And next time, could you
make it easy for us, learn to host a delicious dinner?

83 Felix describes his underground
Chancellery, 1940

The letters come continuously from Holland in one
"long cry of distress". Impossible not be whipped

into a kind of frenzy to help. But I can choose only
the most pressing. When H's illness is most acute,

he knows his total dependence on me for deliverance.
At his most human then, this otherwise impenetrable

block of a man. I appeal to his feelings of gratitude
and friendship. I must be sparing and discern this

exact combination of factors, and only then suggest
names of my Dutch 'friends' or 'colleagues' or

'patients' who have been arrested. Once the attack
is over he is totally unmoved by any plea of mine.

Then the only thing that works is to manipulate
his desire for history to think well of him – "Great

men of history," I tell him, "are strong and courageous
but also magnanimous." I need to lay it on with a trowel;

experience has shown the exact degree of flattery
to apply. He replies: "My dear Herr Kersten,

you are my only friend, my Buddha, the only man
who can understand me as well as heal me."

Basking in both release from the pincer pain and
my sensitive understanding of him, he summons

Brandt to give him more names. I rejoice for every
one which makes the list! As I pass through Rudi's

office he whispers another warning to be careful –
"Heydrich," he says, "is just waiting for his chance."

84 A cartolina from Felix
Berlin, 1940

Cara,

Three months seems a very long time. But I will return on the 15th to treat the Conte. Will you come direct to my hotel (I take a suite at The Westin Excelsior) and join me for dinner?

L'amore da Flick

85 Felix works hard
Wilmersdorf, Berlin, 1940

I almost sink under the volume of correspondence
from my Dutch compatriots. Of course it is nothing

compared to the horror of their lives under Nazi
occupation, suffering their friends and loved ones

being snatched away from them for no reason,
lives under threat. This is from my current working

list: Mr Röell, former Commander-in-Chief
of the Dutch Army. Mr Colijn, Dutch Prime Minister.

Mrs Van Deyck and Baroness Heemstra. Mr Plesman,
Chief of KLM (Royal Dutch Airlines). H van Royen,

Mr Jacob de Graeff, G J Hintzen, Baron von Strium,
Dr Jan Paul Bannier, Mr F A J Deinum, Mr Clavareau

and Mr Wilkins. Usually I wait until just the right
psychological moment, when H is feeling magnanimous.

That is when I have most success. But sometimes
the death threat is imminent, I cannot afford to wait.

On occasion Himmler screams at me and goes into
a mad rage, accusing me of "sympathising with swine"

or some such. But I am used to riding that storm;
it does nothing to deter me. Regardless, the list grows.

86 Felix talks about the sacred interregna
Wilmersdorf, Berlin, 1940

I can thank Dr Ko's style of massage
for the chances that talking to H

in-depth brings. Usually when
a session first begins, he is locked

inside pain. No reaching him until
I find the vortices, liberate the torsioned

force. I grip and grapple with his guts
and then we pause. Both of us

need to gather energy and only then,
in those sacred interregna, can he

marshal any sense. Mostly he floats
then, high from being free from pain.

He offers gratitude, occasionally
delirious with thanks, willing to do

his best for me. It is in these spaces
I make my requests for clemency.

87 Felix keeps his nerve
Felix's apartment, Wilmersdorf, Berlin, January 1941

Rudi has been warning me that Heydrich will take
revenge for going over his head with the Dutch.

Today he does, ending months of suspense. That
was a relief at least. Two uniformed Gestapo agents

turn up at 6 am when I am still in my pyjamas.
Does H know of their visit – has he sanctioned it?

Or is Heydrich just trying it on? I sweat that
uncertainty. They ask me if I treat Jews. I confirm

I do, feeling that this discussion will resolve it
with the Gestapo once and for all. *"Verboten!"*

They almost spit out their disgust. "It is *verboten* for
German doctors to treat Juden! You place yourself

outside German law," is how they put it. "But I am
not a German doctor," I respond, consternation

immediately obvious on their faces. "I am a Finnish
National, travel with a Finnish passport and work

as a Finnish Councillor of Medicine," I say. Producing
my Finnish passport proves it. One agent splutters

an embarrassed apology, the other informs me they
had been given false intelligence. In her rooms

Elisabeth sleeps through the whole episode! I wake
her and she puts on the pot for Kaffee.

88 Felix describes Himmler's rage
Berlin, January 1941

When H hears of my
early morning Gestapo

visit he is livid that I
have been targeted

by his detractors
and juniors. He orders

I not be further molested …
under any circumstances!

89 Felix discovers Hitler's plan for the Dutch people

Chancellery, 1 March 1941

In a time of many shocking occurrences I am shocked
anew to read some of H's secret documents. Brandt

shows me the file as a favour. H's delay today gives me
the opportunity to read it: 43 typed sheets in a folder

marked STRENG GEHEIM – TOP SECRET. Hitler's plan
to resettle 8,200,000 Dutch people, in Lublin,

Poland. I have to bite down my expostulation – rein
myself in. The horrible scale and scope of it. Holland's

wonderful farming land, its proximity to England, Hitler
claims, must be settled by pure Aryans. Surely it is just

a monstrous harebrained scheme … but the plans
are so detailed – they specify trains, ships and buses

to transport the sick, elderly and children – while able-
bodied women and men, will be force-marched

across the whole of Europe under guards with whips
and rifles. They have planned the power plants

needed, building materials required. Only they call
it *abwandern*, to be 'made' to go … even the language

is forked. The execution of these plans will begin –
as a grotesque gift – on Hitler's birthday April 20.

Just seven weeks away. Can they really? I am sick
with fear for my friends. Hitler has put H entirely

in charge and – most shocking of all – he is to ensure
that no Dutch Jew will reach their destination!

90 Felix works on Himmler I
Wilmersdorf apartment, Berlin, 2 March 1941

How can I sleep? The horror of what they
are proposing goes round and round. I stay

up late talking with Elisabeth. All night I try
to work out a plan, quail at how monstrous

Hitler's vision is. I am no clearer in the morning
than when I left H's rooms, bamboozled, last

night. When I arrive for our morning appointment
I contrive to get H to admit to it. I tell him I have

overheard Heydrich and Rauter in the Officers'
Kantine. H is on a hair trigger – everything

seems to enrage him. He is furious that Heydrich
and Rauter have such loose tongues, then

expresses indignation that at the very mouth
of the German Rhine, on the very coast of the German

North Sea, there is a country hostile to the Reich,
friendly to England! He is apoplectic. What pressure

he is under – his first big project for Hitler
and he's terrified of failing! None of which helps

his nerves. I have an unusually hard time getting
his system to settle down. I poke and prod, sustain

force on the most recalcitrant of knots. Eventually
loosening occurs. It gives me an idea. Obviously

the work tension affects his health. If I can play
on the hypochondria lurking just below the surface

of his mind ... the only strategy I can think of ...
perhaps ... I can worry him out of compliance.

91 Felix works on Himmler II
Bruck, Austria, 2 March 1941

H is getting worse. I follow him, on his orders,
to Bruck in Styria – his headquarters in Austria.

He is involved in military matters but constantly
at the back of his mind is how he must arrange

the Dutch deportation. There am I, always
harrying where I see room for it. During breaks

in the session, I tell him many times I worry
for him, fear his health will not bear the weight.

I feed the spectre of failing his beloved Führer –
the ghost who stands at the bottom of the bed

and mocks him while I treat. It follows him
around, does not let up. Beneath his eyes

are darkened bruises from lack of sleep –
his nerves in a dreadful state. As are mine.

All I can do at night is reach my armchair
and collapse into its welcome girth.

92 Himmler's sympathetic nerve speaks
Chancellery, 1941

Sympathetic he
is not! Not a single

sympathetic bone
in his body. That's

the point. Oh, ja,
he cares for his

children and wife
(although that

does not stop him
enjoying his mistress

when he can find
time for her), is

a genial, generous
host. But sympathy?

Nein, I truly do not
think him capable

of that. Too pedantic,
petrified to let his

Führer down, frankly,
far too cruel. Is it

any wonder I, his
so-called sympathetic

nerve, am forced so
often into monstrous

contortions
of protest?

93 Elisabeth ruminates
Felix's apartment, Wilmersdorf, Berlin, April 1941

I have never seen Felix so upset and need to take him
    firmly in hand. "Listen to me," I say.
    "You will sit in the chair and take
    hold of yourself!"

He has been pacing and talking himself into a state.
    "We will eat and you will return to Chancellery
    and treat The Herr as usual. That is the only
    way you can help the Dutch."

He obeys like a child but when it is time to leave,
    he recoils, exclaiming: "I shall not go!
    Whatever happens I cannot have
    anything more to do with those people!"

I work on him again, soothing, admonishing, finding
    the right words to convince him.
    By the time he leaves he is somewhat
    restored and without
    yet knowing how it will be done,
    is once again determined to find
    a way to persuade Himmler to desist.

94 Felix is foxy with his words
Chancellery, 16 April 1941

Three times in one day – surely a record!
Colic is too mild a word for how cruelly

behaved his innards are. Broken by his pain,
he pleads, desperate for release. I pummel him

back into the land of humans. But, I say, unless
he eases up, my treatments will soon fail him.

No less than the truth – he will need his all
to ensure the Waffen SS are battle-ready.

An open secret that Wehrmacht troops mass
along the Russian border. A big offensive

is all the talk in the Kantine. My time is now.
I grow foxy with my words, seem to offer

moral support. "Obviously," I tell him, sincerity
oozing from my tone, "you must be well enough

to do all that's necessary for the war. Maybe other
things are not needed just now. Dutch deportation,

for instance," I seem to just stumble across this
possibility, "surely it could be left until after

the fighting finishes? In any case will you not
need resources for other arenas? Go to Hitler

at once," I grow bold in my helpful healer guise,
"and tell him – it is just not possible." I time

my treatment to be at its most painful apex,
keeping him suspended on the very edge,

until he agrees. He is panting, only just coping.
"I shall do what you say, dear Doktor Kersten,"

he says, opposition at last defeated. He slides
down the other side of pain, glides into full

27 March 1941

**Führer Directive
No. 25 (Also
known as the
April War)**

Implemented on
6 April 1941.
Germany attacks
Yugoslavia and
Greece.

gratitude, the humanising influence of deliverance.
I walk back to my apartment with a subtle spring

in my step, feeling at last some measure of hope
that the terrible fate of the Dutch may be averted.

95 Felix expresses his relief
Gut Hartzwalde, 21 April 1941

I am driven home, feeling jubilant.
H has told me the project is deferred!

When I reach Hartzwalde I pick
a posy of snowdrops and crocus

to put in crystal before my portrait
of Queen Wilhelmina and Prince

Hendrik. Not only has H done as he
said he would but Hitler has agreed!

To spare her, preserve the sanctuary
of Hartzwalde, I tell Irm nothing

of my ordeal. When I shut the door
on the evening, just for tonight, I shut

out Berlin, H, the war and the whole
human debacle unfolding across Europe.

96 Irmgard expresses her relief
Gut Hartzwalde, 21 April 1941

I cannot quite put my finger
on it but tonight Flick is better
than he has been for weeks.
A softened crease between
his brows, lightness in his step,

laughter when he plays with
Ulf and Arno, able to talk
without impatience. I remain
in the dark about the burden
but I give thanks for its passing.

97 Felix's relief doesn't last long
Heydrich's Office, Chancellery, 14 May 1941

I have just heard that Hitler has ordered all the doctors
who treated Hess to be arrested – quacks, astrologers,

fortune tellers, and me – his masseur! Hess was Hitler's
favourite Lieutenant and they are appalled, reeling

from his flight, worried he will have given away State
secrets. But I think they want revenge for his solo act.

Heydrich has called me in at 1500 hours today.
I fear my fate. When I treated Hess for Nazi-belly,

he told me he would do something truly great
for the Reich, but gave no details. I try to find H

before my appointment but he and Rudi have left
for Munich, incommunicado. Worry tightens my guts.

I tell the Duty Officer it is crucial the Reichsführer
knows that Heydrich is poised to arrest me.

He promises to do his best while Heydrich keeps
me waiting. When I try to leave the room to ask

a staffer where he is, I find the door locked against me.
I have to use all my training to step back from panic,

calm my ragged breath. Unless H calls to vouch
for me this could be it … Eventually Heydrich sweeps

into the room, all elegance and steel-blue courtesy.
He questions me about Hess and though I tell him

Hess told me nothing, he prods and probes. He bats me
around, telling me all the reasons he distrusts me.

Only his mouth smiles – this is interrogation
and it is rigorous. He tells me he will have to

arrest me as he believes nothing I say. He says
he knows it was I who talked Himmler out of

the Dutch deportation. Here it comes, I think,
waiting for the move that will finish me off.

He delights in playing cat and making prisoners
play mouse. I try to keep my calm, regulate

my breath. We go over the same ground again
and again, at his leisure: the Dutch situation,

what Hess told me, what connections I have to Jews,
whether I am a British spy. After many hours

I am wound as tight as a spring can wind. Feigning
nonchalance, I suggest he asks H directly for proof

of my innocence. An outer office phone takes
him from the room. H coming to my aid, I hope.

He returns, fixes me with those ice-blue eyes, leaves
an uncomfortable silence … "You are free to go.

Himmler has just telephoned to me. He will vouch
for your loyalty to the Führer himself. I am therefore

forced to let you go … Don't worry, we will meet again."
I leave on shaking legs, like so many others exiting

that dreaded building, needing to walk many blocks
before I clear my system of the metallic taste of terror.

98 Felix rejoins the circus
On board Sonderzug Heinrich, 21 June 1941

H is on the move again
and again I am ordered

to rejoin the circus.
Trapped like a bear

in a cage and the thought
of Officers' jubilation

over breaches in the Russian
line revolts me. I spend

two long lonely months
at the front – treating H

every day, sometimes
more than once, desperate

and on edge without
restorative *Wochenende*

at Hartzwalde, without
Irm, Elisabeth and the boys.

22 June 1941

Operation Barbarossa

German code name for the invasion of the Soviet Union. The winter of 1941–42 is bitterly cold and German soldiers unprepared. "Frost singes skin and flesh, like a sort of cold fire, so that it simply died and fell from men's bodies. Eyelids, ears, noses and lips were stripped from faces; hands lost their fingers; bodies their arms and legs. Even sexual organs have been known to freeze like icicles and snap off." Thousands of German soldiers die of or are debilitated by injuries caused by the cold.

Unterkühlungs-versuche **(Freezing and hypothermia experiments)**

Conducted by Dr Rascher, reporting to Himmler at Birkenau, Dachau and Auschwitz, simulating the Eastern Front. Victims are put in a vat of icy water or outside, naked in sub-zero temperatures.

99 Felix witnesses cowardice
On board Sonderzug Heinrich, June 1941

Never brave, always the first
to seek the security of his shelter

once the Russian planes begin
their nightly sortie and the siren

starts to scream. H runs helter-skelter,
fear making him more ungainly

than ever. No thought for the safety
of his men. The ridiculous sight

of his white flannel nightshirt flapping
against his skinny, chicken-bone legs.

100 SS officer Erich von dem Bach-Zelewski explains

Minsk, Soviet Belorussia, August 1941

The Reichsführer orders me to organise an Aktion
for him to witness. He wants to assess our efficiency.

Normally the Einsatzgruppen are not quite sober so I
worry they will mess it up. I worry non-stop. I walk

around in misery for days. We stand together at the pit-
mouth. As soon as the first shots are fired and the victims

collapse, Himmler himself blanches and sways.
He almost faints when blood and brain matter spatter

his greatcoat. I grab his sleeve lest he fall into the writhing
mass grave with the rest. Bedlam reigns; the marksmen

did not shoot true, victims scream amid further gun
bursts, Himmler rants like a madman, hurling abuse

for their poor aim, their shocking execution. However
much he targets them, the failure of nerve was clearly

his. No wonder they they are mocking him as 'Reichsheini'.
I hear afterwards he orders in future women and children

will be killed in gas vans. His dressing down of me –
and worse – he saves for the privacy of his field office.

101 Words from an SS Officer
Minsk, December 1941

***Einsatzgruppen Aktion* (mobile killing unit)**

"The realisation of what was really happening
only dawned on me very slowly, over a period

of weeks and months, like a great red sun that
rose within me, centimetre by centimetre, until

it flooded my entire being with its bloody radiance.
And what was true for me was true for us all.

For it was only in those last months of 1941 and
early '42 that what people now call the Holocaust

gradually emerges from countless more or less
random acts of violence to become something

very different; a coherent program of extermination,
planned with extraordinary precision and detail."

102 Felix is horrified
Chancellery, 11 November 1941

H is in a strange melancholy mood when I arrive
this morning. The war with Russia falters and Britain

is more tenacious than they thought. But it is not
this which weighs the Reichsführer down. "Are you

in pain?" I ask as he prepares for treatment. Before
he lies down, he folds his glasses and places them

carefully on the nightstand, looking myopically
towards me, always more vulnerable without

the scant protection they offer. At first he cannot
say. I reassure him of my care – "I am your doctor

and friend, everything that concerns you concerns
me too, because it affects your nerves." Now he will

not make eye contact, his shoulders droop – I have
never seen him so full of despair! "It is the Jews,"

he eventually says. "After France falls to us, Hitler offers
peace to Britain, several times, but each time, because

they are controlled by Jews, they reject his offer.
I tell you, the Jews cause the rottenness on which

they thrive!" He builds up a head of steam, repeating
anti-Semitic views I have already debated with him

many times. No point arguing when he is irrational.
I let him continue until he is done. "The damage they

have done in robbing nations of their heritage! The millions
of dead caused by the Jews must be held against them!

Hitler has realised that there will be no peace as long
as they rule. So … he has ordered me to … liquidate

them." "What do you mean … liquidate them?" I reply,
mind reeling. "I mean that this race must be exterminated

Kiev, Ukraine,
29-30
September 1941

Babi Yar

In a ravine outside
town, as part
of Operation
Barbarossa, on
the most sacred
Jewish day, Yom
Kippur (Day
of Atonement),
Einsatzgruppen
and local
collaborators
shoot 33,771
Jews in a single
operation. Apart
from the Death
Camps, this will
become the
biggest single Nazi
atrocity.

3 September
1941

The first test gas
murders start at
Auschwitz.

Pharaonengräber
(Pharoah's Tombs)

Graves at mass-
murder sites.

once and for all! The tragedy of greatness is to have
to trample corpses," he adds in a pathetic self-pitying coda.

"But Herr Himmler … you can not … what
a monstrous idea! What suffering, misery you would

cause!" I pause to take breath and gather my wits – I
know the Nazis have crazy megalomaniacal ideas,

know they dreamed up annihilating the Dutch
Jews just a few months back, but this surpasses

anything I can conceive! There is no response
I can find equal to the depravity of the man,

the men, these so-called rulers of this so-called
Tausendjähriges Reich. Gott im Himmel, help us all.

CHAPTER IV

103 Himmler pontificates on pest control
Chancellery, 1941

Man has an obligation to
defend himself against

lice and bedbugs, against
vermin and parasites of all

kinds – crucial principle of
a civilised society. "Anti-

Semitism is exactly the same
as delousing. Getting rid

of vermin is not a question
of ideology at all but only

a matter of maintaining
strictest social cleanliness."

104 Irmgard speaks
Gut Hartzwalde, November 1941

I know that Felix often protects us from what happens
outside Hartzwalde's gates, and I am grateful he keeps
the boys safe but sometimes I wish I knew what worries
him. I read the paper and hear about the many enemies
of the Reich. You have to admire the Nazis their resolve.

But the Gestapo are cruel and The Herr's role … well,
to say it worries me is understatement. I know what
reserves of energy it requires of Felix to treat him.
It tells – often he comes home so exhausted he can
hardly hold his body upright. But this time it is not

just physical tiredness – I know how that affects him.
This is different. Something weighs him down.
Restless, he roams the forest paths for hours; distracted
and distant from all that usually brings him joy. Not even
the beloved balm of Hartzwalde does the trick.

105 Himmler describes his gift card index
Chancellery, December 1941

Auntie of the Presents is my pet name for Fräulein
Lorenz, meine wunderbare SS record-keeper of gifts.

Common courtesy, natürlich, to know the gifts you
give and get. My records serve the SS, serve the

Reich! I have her scrupulous with details. Birth-year,
rank, Party number, Kinder, Frau's maiden name.

Where he lives and how to name him – du or Dear
Party Member, plain Party Member or Herr. An edge

if you get it right. You can be sure I keep an eagle-eye
on my associates. Nothing much escapes my ken

or goes to waste. Even how they pen their *Dankesbrief*
reveals character. My graphologists interpret hand-

writing, what it tells of strength and weakness. You
never know which intelligence will work for you.

I give modest gifts – so the Volk do not get greedy:
SS calendars, porcelain figures from the Allach factory.

For the Damen in these slender days, half a kilogram
of Schokolade, Kaffee, tinned sardines, bacon rashers.

At Yuletide I pen the words myself – "Danke for the help
you give the Reich. Seasons Greetings. Heil Hitler!"

Words from the
Nazi lexicon,
Poland, 7
December 1941

***Chelmno*
(Chelmno
Concentration
camp)**

The first test
gassing of Jews in
gas vans occurs.
The victims are
greeted on arrival
by the Camp
Commandant
dressed as the
squire of the
Estate in feather
hat, jackboots
and smoking a
pipe. Prisoners
are told they
will be treated
fairly and well
fed in exchange
for labour. They
are led into the
'washrooms'
which are in fact
gas vans. A driver
drives them to the
forest, where they
are poisoned by
gas; dead after ten
minutes.

***Miefmobil* (Stale-
air mobile)**

Poison-gas truck.

106 Felix wants them to have suffered
Gut Hartzwalde, 1942

There is no consolation in them going to hell,
even if they burn. There is no help if karma

punishes them in a next life, should there be
one. You want them to have suffered while

they lived, in the life where they did the harm.
You want some huge payback for what they

bring – black and voracious – into the world.
It is nowhere near enough, but consider their

bodies – the rebellious writhe and gripe
of intestines, huddled in stomach's dark cave.

Hitler resorting to quacks and his daily dose –
capsules of processed soldier's shit. H's stomach

forcing him unconscious, rheumatism, headaches. Von Ribbentrop's litany: headaches,

partial loss of vision, stomach cramps. Ley's
excruciating pancreas. Schellenberg's agonising

stomach. Hess's aches and pains. For all their
Aryan perfection, they are a bunch of crocks.

In some hidden psychic corner, part of them protests.
Men whose guts cannot digest their deeds.

107 Felix grieves the death of his father
Gut Hartzwalde, January 1942

At a time when so many suffer, I have a small
personal sorrow. After ninety-one years of daily toil

my Vati's body has finally quit. Wonderful
companion for Irm while I am repeatedly

away, major support in running the estate.
Vater-figure for my boys – teaching them

woodcraft, animal husbandry, supervising
their lessons. She – and they – who share

the daily round, may miss him more than I.
But Vati was my model and I grieve him.

Words from the
Nazi lexicon, 7
December 1941

***Nacht-und- Nebel-
Erlass* (Night-and-
Fog Decree)**

Persons who were
believed to have
endangered the
security of the
German State or the
occupying force are
secretly transported
to Germany where
they disappear
without a trace.
Relatives and friends
of the people who
vanish into the 'night
and fog' are denied
any knowledge of
their whereabouts
or fate.

The name of the
decree is from a spell
in Wagner's opera
Das Rheingold.

7 December 1941

Pearl Harbor

Japan stages a
surprise attack on
American military
installations in the
Pacific.

Words from the
Nazi lexicon,
20 January 1942

***Endlösung der
Judenfrage (Final
Solution of the
Jewish Question)***

The major focus
for the Wannsee
Conference (Berlin)
attended by all the
major Schutzstaffel
(SS) chiefs. This was
a euphemism for
the elimination of
Jews in German-
held territories.
Under the control of
Obergruppenführer
Reinhard Heydrich,
Himmler's emissary.
The purpose of the
conference is to
ensure cooperation
with the already-
planned Final
Solution.

January 1942

Mass killings of
Jews using Zyklon
B, a cyanide-based
pesticide, begin at
Auschwitz-Birkenau
concentration camp.

108 Felix explains how the *Bibelforscher* come to Hartzwalde

Gut Hartzwalde, July 1942

The loss of Vati's work on the farm
tells, and the number who have enlisted

means this harvest will be short of hands.
Neighbouring farmers tell me they use inmates

from the Camps. Ravensbrück is close
so I ask H if he would permit some prisoners

to labour on our farm. I add the proviso:
there be no guards or dogs – I know the Nazis!

He agrees to send ten female *Bibelforscher* –
Jehovah's Witnesses. They arrive this morning,

in a shocking state. There has been talk and enough
of H's rants to know that Nazi hatred abounds

but I believed what I had been told: that the
Camps are for re-education purposes, strict

and regimented, natürlich. Nothing prepares me
for the sight of these wretches: pitiful, bedraggled,

reduced in every conceivable way. I listen to their
horror stories of starvation-level rations, ill-

treatment at the hands of the guards, overwork
to collapse-point. Imprisoned only because their

religion forbids them to make the Nazi salute –
they acknowledge God, not man, as the highest.

Two have been imprisoned for seven unbearable
years. How did they survive? I am horrified to

the point of feeling ill and walk around all day
in a kind of bilious trance of incomprehension.

109 Irm sees with her own eyes
Gut Hartzwalde, July 1942

I cannot believe how far their bones stick out –
agony for them just to shuffle one foot in front
of the other. Such strong women reduced to
skeletons – I am shocked beyond measure.
I slaughter some fowl, make healing broths,

and loaves and loaves. Though ravenous
they can hardly keep food down. My huge pot is
constantly on the stove for hot water so they
can bathe, soak their poor battered bodies and
remove some of the grime and infestation. I find

old garments until we buy replacements for their
rags. The boys' eyes are huge, their normal chatter
silenced – they could not be more helpful, Ulf
chops and Arno carries wood for the pile. Felix
walks around in a daze; for all his previous Nazi

exposure, this has rocked him. I choke on
the multiple, grievous assaults they have endured,
and when they offer their heartfelt gratitude …
I have to turn my head so they do not see my
tears. What sort of a people have we become?

Words from the
Nazi lexicon

**Schmuckstücke
(Trinkets)**

A vicious term
used by camp
guards for the
female prisoners
on the verge of
starvation and/
or disease at
Ravensbrück
concentration
camp.

110 Felix decides he has to do more
Gut Hartzwalde, July 1942

I am rocked. Is this really what
the Nazis are up to, behind

our backs? Not just Jews in their
sights, as if that were not bad

enough. Overnight the world
has become unrecognisable.

The only way I can see to help
is to do more. But what? Firstly

I ask H to release another twenty
Jehovah's Witness women to labour

on our farm. 'Happy' does no justice
to how they feel to leave the foetid,

deadly environs of the camp,
to come to the fresh air and safe

haven of Hartzwalde. Nor to how
relieved Irm and I feel to give

real help to some of those in need.
The women know the threat we

face in harbouring them; will do
anything to protect us. We have

done a tiny good thing – a teaspoonful
in an ocean of suffering. Impossible

not to feel dwarfed by the need.
Next time I treat H, I decide, I will

tackle him directly about the horror
of what happens in the camps.

111 Felix tackles Himmler
Field HQ, Zhitomir, Ukraine, 5 July 1942

Fortuitous that H has ordered me to accompany him
to field HQ where I treat him many times each day

and can prosecute my plan. Tonight after dinner I steel
myself: "Reichsführer, is it true that men and women

are systematically tortured to death in the concentration
camps? I do not like to mention it to you, but I have

received some information which makes me ask." He
lets out a laugh: "Come now, Herr Kersten, you are falling

for allied propaganda!" "It is not a matter of propaganda
at all, but facts from a very reliable source," I shoot back,

adept as any sportsman. "What source is that?" he parries.
"I met two Swiss journalists at the Finnish Embassy

who were en route to Sweden." I begin the story
I devised to protect my Jehovah's Witness sources.

"They have many photographs bought from SS guards."
(I hear in the Reichsführer's Mess that SS

camp guards are ordered to photograph and film
all executions and tortures. Such barbarism …

I only just manage to bite back bile). H immediately
sits up on his camp bed, and that abrupt movement

tells me that what I had hoped was not true, is indeed
true. "Where are they now, those journalists?" he fires

at me. "I must immediately get in touch with them
and buy back those photographs! Absolutely

imperative!" I reply that they would have left Germany
already, would have arrived in Sweden. I add that

the stories about the camps are not just enemy
propaganda. H sighs. "I admit," he says soberly,

The Rasse- und Siedlungshauptamt-SS (SS Race and Settlement Main Office) (RuSHA)

Established by Himmler in 1931. A 1942 pamphlet states that "subhumans only seemed biologically similar to Aryans because they had 'hands, feet and a kind of brain, with eyes and a mouth'. But they [a]re 'a completely different, dreadful creature, only a rough copy of a human being, with human-like facial traits but morally and mentally lower than any animal. Within this creature there is a fearful chaos of wild, uninhibited passions, nameless destructiveness, the most primitive desires, the nakedest vulgarity. For all that bear a human face are not equal. Woe to him who forgets it.'"

"regrettable things do happen on occasion ..."
Minimising of course, and it gives me confirmation

I dreaded having. All the fears kept at bay now surge
into the forefront of my mind. My whole being twists

with revulsion and helplessness. I do not know
how, all I know is that I must find ways to do more.

112 Felix hopes to make another ally
Field HQ, Zhitomir, July 1942

I feel my fetters even more here
than on the Sonderzug. H has

made a house available though
I – the only civilian – have no

liberty to walk around so close
to the war zone. For exercise,

under armed guard, desultory
circuits of the barbed-wire-

enclosed rifle range. At my wits'
end with boredom, on edge

because of the scheming
and manoeuvring, I am relieved

when H lines up Walter Schellenberg
from SS Foreign Intelligence

for me to treat. A favourite of H's,
he is a detractor of Ribbentrop

and, like me, considers
Kaltenbrunner a sworn enemy –

perhaps we will get on. His
complaint – wouldn't you know

it – stomach cramps – another
Nazi with his gizzards in a stew!

113 Schellenberg recounts first meeting with Kersten

Field HQ, July 1942

Oh mein Gott! Kersten weighs almost 250 pounds
and when he puts his bulk into the massage his force

is fierce. Agony when he plunges hands into me!
Nothing prepares me for the torture of having my

tormented ligatures undone. He delves, manhandles
the ropes my intestines make until they are persuaded

to let go. And I … I breathe out a long held-in exquisite
groan of pain. Afterwards we talk politics – how Himmler

considers the Führer's prospects. We start out careful
but each disclosure confirms us as allies. We think

Himmler can be coaxed and flattered into usurping
the Führer. We both see he is transparent with vanity.

Perhaps we can cajole him into allowing us to negotiate
peace with Britain. We agree to work together. Treason,

should either of us be caught. Later, I broach Himmler
himself with questions about the Führer's plans. I tell

him straight I have no confidence in where the Reich
heads, expound my ideas for negotiated peace. He rants

at first, then, thinking, chews his nails and fiddles with
his death's-head ring. He calms down enough to seriously

consider his plight, come a vanquished Reich. Eventually
he grants me full and complete authority to proceed.

I do not trust him, of course, prevarication and uncertainty
his hallmarks. But I am encouraged. History will likely

remember me for negotiations such as this but alongside
the sober, dangerous game of brinkmanship, I have

Kersten's massages, daily. By day five I am a new man.
Pain-free! Even Himmler notices my appearance

of deliverance. Pain was a taken-for-granted part of life;
treatment under Kersten becomes a highlight of my war.

114 Felix explains the *Svenska Tändsticks AB*

Schloss Aigen, Himmler's Headquarters, July 1942

We have moved again, stationed now near Salzburg
with no more liberty for me – one field HQ as dull,

grey and soldier-filled as another. Food is daily
digestive torment. At least I have projects

to work on. My lawyer friend, Dr Carl Langbehn,
has enlisted my help in the case of some

Swedish industrialists and engineers from
the Swedish Matchstick Company arrested

by the Gestapo in Warsaw, accused of espionage.
I present the case to H and he gets Rudi

to investigate. He will meet with company
executives, Herren Brandin und Möller, to hear

their side. I have coached H to have an eye to
how history can be shaped to present him in

a better light. He has taken the bait, is interested
although he warns me that ever-uncooperative

Foreign Minister Ribbentrop will need to know.
Perhaps a long shot but many others have been

equally unlikely. And it gives me something other
than pumped-up Nazis and poor fare to ponder.

115 Himmler describes training of concentration-camp guards

Field HQ, Zhitomir, July 1942

What H told to me as part of the treatment yesterday
was utterly repellent. He explained in his most school-

teacherly manner, with no awareness of how horrific
what he said was: "If an SS soldier infringes the rules

he is brought before a court-martial and given the
choice to be punished and have the punishment

recorded on his file, forever preventing promotion.
Or he can go to a concentration camp as a warder

with all privileges and freedom regarding the prisoners.
He chooses the latter and once there his superior officer

asks – note – asks, not orders him, to torture then kill a
prisoner. He is given another choice: to be sent back

to his unit with even heavier punishment or to carry out
the task. The first time he tortures and kills he is

coerced into it, but most develop a taste for it, and
begin to boast of their success. Then we have to

liquidate them because this is too early to become
public. More come to fill their position …" Once I

recover a little I respond: "… you know you will go
down in history as the greatest murderer of them all!"

I cut his treatment short, disgusted, and cannot wait
to leave the man, to leave the building, to leave

the whole Nazi *Weltanschauung*. I am trembling so
fiercely I can hardly find my coat sleeves. I return to

my quarters. I wash and wash, trying to cleanse
myself of the malodorous stain left clinging to my skin.

116 Felix discovers something about his adopted country
Field HQ, Zhitomir, July 1942

To my horror I learn that Hitler is going to ask
Finland to hand over their entire Jewish population;

their 2,000 are intended to suffer Endlösung alongside
other European Jews. H tells me that Hitler has

ordered him to fly to Helsinki to make the demand.
He wants me to go with him, claiming his need

for physical therapy whilst he handles such a demanding
matter. I argue for my adopted country, its Jews. He

shoots my argument down: "Don't talk nonsense, Herr
Kersten. Your country's independence will only last

as long as it suits the Führer's purpose. Germany is the
strongest country in the world. No power on earth can

overcome us!" He reminds me that Finland is dependent on
Germany's grain; bread stocks will only last three weeks.

Germany will not make the delivery, he threatens, unless
Finland hands over her Jews! Perhaps going with him

is opportunity to shape events in some small way,
although I fear matters are already beyond my influence.

117 Felix ruminates
Felix's apartment, Wilmersdorf, Berlin, July 1942

I carry awareness of each prisoner
on whose behalf I work in a small

tight pocket in my mind. As each
person is freed from custody,

the stitches dissolve, the fabric unravels
from its pucker. Enormous liberation

for them, welcome release for me.
Today Dutch Prime Minister Colijn

was discharged from jail, two years after
I started working on his case.

118 Felix accompanies Himmler to Finland

German Embassy, Helsinki, July 1942

H and I meet Foreign Minister Witting and President
Ryti in the Embassy gardens. Roses of every hue

bloom profusely and their heady fragrance wafts
around us, unlikely accompaniments. A glorious

summer day, marred totally by our mission. It seems
impossible to turn our task to good. Though H

is putting on a bold international diplomacy show,
I know he is anxious about the impression he makes

by the way his hand hovers in front of his face,
contriving to hide his receding chin. Pathetic gesture

from an essentially weak individual, hollow with
insecurity. The horrendous paradox of the man!

As Hitler's lackey, he is crazy enough to offer Finland
half of Sweden to rule, for all the world like a child

playing board games! I am embarrassed just to be
seen in his presence, wish the earth would open,

swallow me whole. Seeing him outside Germany,
out of his niche, makes his mannerisms, his pumped-up

power plays transparent. He makes his 'offer' despite
the Swedes coming to Finland's aid in the Winter War

with Russia in '39! Madness to ignore international
friendships and to think he can carve up Europe

on Hitler's megalomaniacal whim! He could not have
judged the men or mood more wrongly. Witting,

a model of diplomacy, calmly replies that Finland
has absolutely no ambitions like that. It knocks

the wind out of H's sails and he indicates his wish
for us to leave the gathering shortly afterwards.

Later I am able to arrange secret meetings with Witting.
He is red with outrage at the multiple affronts.

We decide that procrastination is the only way to deal
with the Jewish question. Returning to the hotel I tell H

that surrendering the Jews needs parliamentary approval
and Parliament is in recess until November. Neat sophistry,

which he buys, motivated by his aim of protecting
Finnish strategic value. Later I hear him brief Hitler

over the telephone, who swallows the story that the Finns
accept the principle of surrendering their Jews.

**Schlacht von
Stalingrad (Battle
of Stalingrad)**

The siege of
Stalingrad lasts
for over five
gruelling months
with massive loss
of life. Germany's
defeat here in
'43 becomes
the turning
point of the war.
Afterwards most
Europeans no
longer believe that
Germany will win
the war.

119 Himmler pontificates on good and evil
Field Headquarters, 8 August 1942

"'What you have done in this life will witness for or
against you, inexorably.'" Himmler reads to me

from his vademecum, a small book of homilies
for his guidance. "'As his wife and children welcome

a man ... so on the threshold of another life,
his good deeds await him like friends welcoming

a dear friend.'" "And what about his evil deeds?"
I say, aghast at his lack of self-awareness. "In this

life you have to pay for everything, so why should
you not be presented with a bill in this field too?"

He says it blithely, as if there could be no possible
dispute. "But aren't you often frightened yourself,

Herr Reichsführer," surprised I have to spell it out,
"when you reflect on the things you sometimes

have to do, which one day will be debted against
you?" He replies with great seriousness: "You

oughtn't to look at things from such a limited
egotistical point of view, Herr Kersten ... A man

has to sacrifice himself ... Of course it's pleasanter
to concern yourself with flowerbeds rather than

political dust-heaps and refuse-dumps, but flowers
won't thrive unless these things are seen to. I try

to reach a good compromise in my own life:
I try to help people and do good, relieve

the oppressed and remove injustices wherever
I can. Do you think my heart's in all the things

which have to be done simply for reasons
of state? What I wouldn't give to be Minister

for Religious Matters ... to dedicate myself
to positive achievements only." How he twists

the truth! Anything which enters his belief system's
vortex goes through a twisting tornado, exiting

with every last scrap of logic, morals, scruples
or any of the civilised values, expunged.

120 Felix realises he has to get out
Sometime in 1942

It is a madhouse and I have to get out!
For all the brazen Nazi talk, there never

is going to be any *Tausendjähriges
Reich*. Germany is run by a bunch

of crazy madmen who will not be able
to keep things together for much longer.

I cannot bear it another day! And how
will the Allies judge me? Ensconced

in the Nazis' midst as Reichsführer H's
personal physician, trusted confidant –

what can they think but that I approve,
endorse, at the very least ensure H is

fit for what passes as 'service'? It will
not look good for me. I must get out,

find a way to persuade him to let me,
Irm, Elisabeth and the boys, go. It will

not be easy. He is totally dependent
on me as physician and, alas, as friend.

I need to find a neutral country willing
to take us – Sweden is the only choice.

121 Felix hears more bad news
August 1942

I ask H today if talk I hear is true – that the Nazis
have found another way to depopulate Holland.

In the Kantine I overhear they are buying up
all the black-market food to cause mass starvation.

He replies that it is not only Holland but Belgium
and France as well! I had imagined him somewhat

shame-faced but instead he beams at me, proud
of his simple 'elegant' plan. I argue for the French,

the value of their great culture. "The peasants will
always survive," he replies, dismissively, with a wave

of his hand. "That is what we want, a purely
agricultural France, a milch cow for the Reich."

122 Felix ponders Himmler
Felix's apartment, Wilmersdorf, Berlin, 1942

"The real person
never seems to

reveal himself.
There is never

any hint of openness.
Himmler doesn't

fight, he plots.
The only way

he defends his
so-called ideas

is with guile and
deception. His

methods are
those of a snake

… Himmler's
thinking does

not belong in
the twentieth century.

His character is
medieval, feudal,

Machiavellian,
evil."

123 Felix entertains
Stockholm, September 1942

I love entertaining and host a dinner
in Stockholm for Schellenberg and

Langbehn. What joy to select a menu
without food restrictions – real butter

and Kaffee, creamy Schokolade. Good
company; urbane, entertaining men.

Best of all they are not zealots! Holiday-
like refreshment for the spirits. They

have much in common, will be able
to help one another. All of us desperate

to bring an end to the horror, to pressure
H to depose Hitler or use any other means

we can contrive to secure European
peace. We imbibe the talk, the excellent

food, and wicked black humour at the
Reich's expense – to bolster our resolve.

Words from
the Nazi
lexicon,
Oranienburg,
Germany,
October 1942

***Haus der
schlechte
Ernährung***
**(House of Poor
Nourishment)**
Himmler sets
up the House
to inflict poor
nourishment
on Waffen SS
and police
officers who are
not ensuring
that their own
troops are well-
nourished.

8 November
1942

**Operation
Torch**
The British/
American
invasion of
French North
Africa.

124 Felix talks about Himmler in Italy
Hotel Ambassadore, Rome, October/November 1942

Without needing to exert too much pressure,
the Reichsführer gives me a couple of months'

leave to tend my regular patients in Rome. Ciano
has treatments every day and tells me how very

discontented the Italians grow, tethered to Germany.
When I tell H of their muffled clamours for peace

he joins me in Rome in October, to bolster the Nazi
cause with the top brass. Attending a big reception,

in his best, genial, man-about-town guise,
the Reichsführer holds the floor in a group including

Foreign Minister Ciano, Minister of the Interior
Buffarini and the SS man in the German Embassy

here in Rome, Eugen Dollmann. After complimenting
Ciano on his obviously much improved health, H

praises my skills sky-high, to blushing point.
Jovial, teasing, a rarely-seen side of a usually serious

man, sitting so strangely with the dour, bookish
bureaucrat or the brutal, ruthless Gestapo-head.

125 Himmler talks about Kersten in Italy
Hotel Ambassadore, Rome, October/November 1942

I am praising Herr Kersten's skill with a group
of top-ranking Romans at the reception they

call in our honour. The usually composed Kersten
squirms, affording much entertainment for me.

I tell them I could not live without his treatments.
"But how stubborn he is – a real Finn, as well as

a patriot. Nothing for himself but always he asks
favours for compatriots and friends. What a nuisance,

giving me trouble with his endless lists of names
and requests for mercy – for traitors who thwart

the Führer's will! Dutch, Jewish, German traitors
and criminals one and all! How do I put up with him?"

Our rotund Buddha, he is well aware of his omni-
potence – "Eh, Kersten?" I say, jabbing him in the ribs.

126 Wilhelm Wulff, Astrologer,
describes his first meeting with Felix
Winter 1942

I cannot say he makes a good impression.
A former client takes me to meet him

in his new apartment in Berlin, acquired after
previous Jewish occupants are evicted.

A "pompous" dwelling, full of "ostentatious
elegance". He is sullen, as we are late.

I observe him keenly. "Greedy little eyes …
reminiscent of a child's, peep from his

bloated face. A thyroid case who suffers
from fatty degeneration of the heart.

But despite his enormous girth he is quick
on his feet. His fat grasping hands, covered

with small whitish scars, play continuously
with a pencil. In the terminology of medieval

character assessment, he is phlegmatic
with a sanguine touch. He is extremely

passionate and sensuous, extremely lazy,
extremely vain and ambitious." He has wormed

his way into the inner sanctum by posing
as a harmless masseur, making himself

indispensable to Himmler when all he is committed
to are plans for his own benefit. To make himself

more interesting to Himmler, he wants me
to draw up horoscopes for Himmler

and the Führer. Oh, and while I am at it,
one for himself as well. Jawohl, Herr Kersten!

127 Felix considers Wulff
Felix's apartment, Wilmersdorf, Berlin, Winter 1942

Well, what to make of Herr Wulff?
Zimmermann organises his release

from Fuhlsbüttel where the Gestapo
throw him, along with other occult

practitioners who might have advised
Hess to fly to England. Freed into Herr

Zimmermann's custody, Wulff is an
almost-parolee. Potential leverage

in schemes Schellenberg and I spin?
H believes in the occult arts, fervent

like many top Nazis, despite banning
it for ordinary Volk. As passionate

about astrology as any Christian about
his God. What if we could get Wulff

to doctor H's astrological chart, to suggest:
it is time to be bold That: *peace-making*

actions are now favourable. That: *the stars*
(and any other damn planetary body

Wulff can think of) *are aligned, so*
far-sighted, unprecedented steps

are appropriate, nein, needed. Couched
in astrological jargon, not too specific,

just enough to appear that *The Stars*
push H in the direction Schellenberg

wants him to go – towards peace. Wulff
may not like the interference, may suffer

scruples, but honestly, the time for such
misgivings is well gone. I tell him

to draw up my chart so we can see just
how good an astrologer he really is.

128 Elisabeth keeps a tally
Felix's apartment, Wilmersdorf, Berlin, November 1942

Felix holds many things close to his chest
    but often he needs the pressure-release
    of recounting to me
    details of his day and talks
    with The Herr. What a strange
    enigma the Reichsführer is.

I hear about the brutality he inflicts – people
    just disappear into the great gaping
    mouth of the Gestapo
    never to be heard of again.

Of course we are told the criminals deserve
    their fate. But wirklich, everyone
    knows someone who has disappeared
    with no cause.

The country is in a sorry state under the likes of
    The Herr. But at the same time
    Felix tells me how the man
    is so grateful
    to be freed from pain
    he is happy to release prisoners
    at Felix's behest.

In Felix's hands, one release buys another.
    How to reconcile the paradox
    of the person? Despite the
    good that comes from it,

I do not know how Felix can bring himself to touch him.
    Today's tally:
    Twenty-eight Dutchmen
    Six Germans
    Four Norwegians.
    Another thirty-eight to add to my list.

129 Felix talks about the Führer's health
Chancellery, 12 December 1942

At first in a guarded, anonymous manner and then
clearly, unequivocally, the Reichsführer asks me

to treat the Führer. It seems he was once treated,
successfully it was thought, for syphilis. But

the disease is progressive and he is again suffering
symptoms. So great is H's misery at having to face

this terrifying fact about his beloved master that
he begins to shake in the story's telling. He gives me

a medical file to read and it seems an accurate
diagnosis – the Führer, Great Leader of the Greatest

German Reich, mighty Aryan nation, has the symptoms
of progressive syphilitic paralysis! 'Appalled' does no

justice to how I feel – the world shakes in this madman's trembling hands and Himmler wrings *his* hands.

130 Felix considers strategy
19 December 1942

December
1942

Finland's
Parliament
rejects proposals
to deport
their Jews to
Germany.

I wait, knowing how delicate it is for H to have shared
this 'tragedy' with me. Considerable trust just to broach

the topic. I summon all my skills of silence and
discretion, knowing I can never refer to that discussion

again, must wait until H himself brings it up. But I am
desperate to have my say. Opportunity comes today.

H asks me if I have come up with means to treat Hitler
effectively. All my feverish fears and forebodings take

charge of my tongue and accost the Reichsführer –
"How can you leave Hitler, so compromised, in charge

of the country? The man is sick and will just get sicker,"
I say. Does H not realise the deterioration Hitler will

undergo? I want to shake some sense into his puny,
ailing frame. He has the SS, can he and they not rule?

"Can you not just take command?" My words are not wise
or considered but they are sincere, and H's slumped

shoulders and woebegone demeanour tells me
he at least harbours some of the same considerations.

He allows me significant sway but there comes a point
when he can go no further. "But I cannot, Herr Kersten,

my honour is loyalty. Imagine if the specialists' diagnosis
is wrong. Then I should have overthrown the most brilliant

leader, on the mere suspicion of physicians!" "So you
will abandon the destiny of the whole German people

to a progressive paralytic?" I reply, appalled again,
not even attempting to keep disdain from my voice.

January/February
1943

**The Battle of
Stalingrad** is
reaching its
bloody conclusion
after five months
of fighting. A
German lieutenant
writes:

"The street is no
longer measured
by metres but
by corpses …
Stalingrad is no
longer a town.
By day it is an
enormous cloud of
burning, blinding
smoke; it is a vast
furnace lit by the
reflection of the
flames. And when
night arrives, one
of those scorching,
howling, bleeding
nights, the dogs
plunge into the
Volga and swim
desperately to
gain the other
bank. The nights
of Stalingrad are
a terror for them.
Animals flee this
hell; the hardest
stones cannot bear
it for long; only
men endure."

131 Felix is triumphant
23 December 1942

I have worked hard for six
months, in close communication

with Schellenberg, and today,
at a low ebb, seeing all his hopes

for the Reich disappearing,
H sees fit to grant me my request –

he frees the seven Swedish businessmen
from the Matchstick Company.

Two he releases effective immediately,
and commutes death sentences

for the other five. This has not been
an easy case and I have despaired

at times of a successful conclusion.
Triumphant, I add them to my list.

132 Felix works his magic

Himmler's Headquarters, Hochwald, East Prussia,
February 1943

In the grip of misery, H calls me to him
in Hochwald. Body-cramp mingled with

psychic cramp at the defeat in Stalingrad;
the perfect melancholic malleability to grant

me favours. I have worked on him since
August last year about the French black-market,

repeating arguments which appeal to his prejudices.
Today I reach the apex of persuasion, geared

perfectly to play the pathetic heartstrings of
the man. "Think, Reichsführer," I say, "how painful

it must be for a French mother to see her child
cramped by hunger and to have nothing to give

him to eat." I appeal to sentimentality, vanity.
"In a thousand years, history will speak glowingly

of Reichsführer Heinrich Himmler, celebrate
the generosity of this great German leader."

He cries copious, thin tears which doubtless
do him good. He actually finds his determination

and, resolved, tells Hitler that continuing
to starve the French will feed the Resistance.

This will not serve the Reich. He must have been
as persuasive with Hitler as I with him because

an order has been made in the name of the
Führer himself to cease all black-market buying

and, without my having to lift a finger, these
measures are also extended to Belgium

and Holland. Tonight, temporarily relieved of
crippling concerns, I sleep as an innocent.

3 February 1943

The Wehrmacht
army, under
General Paulus,
surrenders and is
taken into custody
in Stalingrad.
There has been
a loss of an
estimated 250,000
German troops
and between
500,000 and
1,000,000 Red
Army soldiers.
Stalingrad is a
watershed in
terms of public
and Nazi morale.
Germany's
defeat shatters
its reputation for
invincibility.

133 Felix's journal entries
May 1943

Luck is with me. H is greatly afflicted,
his normal resistance, like his body,

collapsed in on itself. He readily agrees
to everything I ask. I save fourteen Dutch

condemned to death. Yesterday it was
three Estonians, two Letts, six Dutch

and one Belgian. The day before I obtain
pardon for forty-two Dutch facing execution.

The Nazis are meticulous with figures,
work in units of tens, hundreds, tens

of thousands of people – my scale is tiny,
my work piecemeal – only perseverance.

134 Irmgard celebrates another birth
Gut Hartzwalde, May 1943

We have had Felix home for two whole weeks –
and Elisabeth with him to care for the other two
boys. It does him good to be relieved for a time
of the Nazi strain and the many demands of *that
man*. During the second week I go into labour.

An old hand now and with Felix's help, our
third son, Andreas, is born – wailing as they
all have done – another strong and lusty male
voice for the Reich. At this rate I will be in line
for the *Mutterehrenkreuz*, the Mother's Cross

of Honour! At least we can feed ours, I do not
know how mothers in cities manage on the
rations imposed. Felix could not be more pleased.
He would have stayed longer but The Herr calls,
requesting his attendance in Berlin, post-haste.

135 Felix talks about peace
Hochwald, June 1943

I am not the only one to seek
all possible openings in the quest

for peace. Many who would not
countenance it before, quick with

accusations of treason, now see
the writing on the wall. Persuaded

by Stalingrad, the bloodthirstiness
of the regime, Hitler's increasingly

erratic leadership. *Teppichbeisser*,
they call him for his rages, throwing

himself on the floor and biting
the carpet! Not just embarrassment,

but serious doubt about his capacity
to rule – is he even sane? My remedy

is to talk peace every chance I get,
in Berlin under the Nazis' nose, with

Swedes and Americans in Stockholm
and in Helsinki with the Government.

136 Felix attends Himmler's crayfish party
Himmler's Villa, Hegewald, Germany, August 1943

At his customary end-of-summer banquet,
H provisions a table, boasting enough bugs

to feed a small battalion. They are piled high
onto plates and platters, courtesy of the poor,

straitened tax-payer who has to foot the bill
for feasting as well as war. The crayfish sit

resplendent in their glistening red armour,
looking military, heraldic; perfect icons

for H's personal predilections. Who can eat
the most crayfish in a single sitting? Each

a spoonful of creamy deliciousness I cannot
get enough of. Bets are laid just for fun.

Perhaps the winner is no surprise if you look
at my girth, judge the quantity my belly can be

persuaded to accommodate. Seventy crayfish later …
ach, okay, I admit that is a slight, but only slight,

exaggeration. The truth? fifty-six crustacea later,
I am replete. Amongst much ribbing and

officers' jocularity, much teasing for my 'over-
estimate', they crown me *King of the Crays*.

July 1943

Wilhelm Wulff
is asked to draw
a horoscope to
find Mussolini,
who has been
abducted.

137 Himmler pontificates on broodmares
Chancellery, Berlin, 1943

Humans can be bred just
as successfully as animals;

we can create a race of men
with superior qualities. If we

look at the latest research on
breeding plants and animals

it is indeed persuasive. I am
convinced that both intellectual

and spiritual traits are inherited.
We mean to perfect this art

and we will do so with the aid
of the Chosen Women, women

who will volunteer their services
to be bred with Aryan heroes.

138 Irmgard derides Himmler's plans
for women

Gut Hartzwalde, 1943

There is talk in the newspapers about The Herr's
plans for women. *Schenk dem Führer ein Kind*
they exhort! *Give a baby as a gift to the Führer!*
I can think of nothing more repugnant! I would
not want anyone to hear me say this (informers

are hidden everywhere) but wirklich! It is one
thing to raise sons, even daughters, for the Reich,
but to set up special breeding centres – that would
be barbaric. He will have a hard job convincing
women like me that we really are broodmares!

139 Felix cooks up a plan with Kivimäki
Berlin, September 1943

Kivimäki says I need to travel to Helsinki to report
about my underground. Before I even think of squaring

it with H, my mind goes to food! We have not been
able to source salmon since last year and I crave its

soft velvet in my mouth. Before I totally lose myself
in fantasy I seek H's approval, simple because

of my citizenship. Arvid Richert, Swedish Minister
in Berlin, gets wind of my plans, requests me to break

my journey in Stockholm for confidential meetings.
What do they want with me? Also, desperate to leave

the Reich, I will be able to explore how to move
my family to Sweden. And … ecstasy to be in a free

and neutral country! Salivating again, this time thinking
of Swedish *choklad*! How to get H's approval

for the Swedish leg … I enlist Kivimäki's help
and we prepare a plan. During the next treatment

I tell H Finland is threatening to enlist me in active service.
He is horrified, cannot countenance seeing a week

through without my massage. I tell him there may be
an alternative, as there are between 5,000 and 6,000

Finnish wounded in Swedish hospitals. If I work there
for two months they will withdraw plans to mobilise me.

A masterful mixture of truth and confabulation.
He does not like it but when I explain that mobilisation

might last until the end of the war he quickly grabs for
the lesser evil, a drowning man. I zip my satchel,

prepare to go, but he clutches my hand, beseeches:
"But you'll come back, you'll be sure to come back?"

CHAPTER V

140 Felix describes his first trip to Stockholm
Stockholm, 30 September 1943

A small family hotel is booked for us in Stockholm.
We have brought only our youngest, Andreas, just

three months old. I am still desperate to get the family
out but I need to handle H's fears. Scare him

too much, he will throw me under house arrest again
and we will never make the move. Whilst negotiating

terms with him, some instinct makes me tell him
I will leave the older boys with Elisabeth at Hartzwalde,

effective hostages against our return. Immediate peace
of mind for him and freedom of movement for us.

I take some crucial papers, incriminating, detailed
journal entries, compromising correspondence

of the whys and wherefores, safe-deposit them
in the capital. Insurance against my future. Not even

Irm knows it is not woollens weighing down my valise!
What a relief to be free of Berlin's heavy brooding

atmosphere, liberated from the soot grey of the buildings,
bedecked with giant red, black and white swastikas.

On our second day Foreign Minister Christian Günther
asks me to visit him at home; so we're not on official

footing. He comes straight to the point, enquires if I will
work with the Swedish Government on a great

humanitarian scheme to free as many as possible from
the camps. A scheme perfectly shaped to my hand.

Over the next few days we nut out details, knock our plan
into shape. *The Günther Plan*, in my own mind at least.

141 Kersten speaks of meeting Hewitt
Stockholm, 3 October 1943

I speak of peace and its possibility every chance I get
inside and outside Germany. I am not the only one.

So much easier here in Stockholm without the
Gestapo breathing down one's neck, eavesdropping

on discussions. You do not realise how wearing
to live under that regime until away, you find your

shoulders drop down and your breath deepen.
How the body holds tension ... Today I meet

an American, Abram Stevens Hewitt, Roosevelt's
special man in Sweden, from the Office of Strategic

Services (OSS). Perhaps through him I can help Finland
make peace ... he has excellent German, so we talk

at depth, easily, getting to know each other and finding
cause for cautious friendship. He tells me his health

is poor, and requests I treat him. I will be happy to
learn more of his views, how we can work together.

142 Irmgard stocktakes
Gut Hartzwalde, November 1943

I enjoy travelling but there is nothing better
than returning home, immersing myself again
in the daily rhythm. We always notice Felix's
father's absence after a trip. But the boys beam,
so eager to see us, and the Jehovah's Witness

women, who ably keep Hartzwalde running
in our absence. As well we are greeted by:
eight horses (including my best big chestnut),
one hundred and twenty hens, twenty-five
cows, twelve sows, and one (enormous) boar.

143 The Reichsführer gives a speech to SS leaders

Poznań, Poland, 4 October 1943

"One principle must be absolute for the SS man: we must
be honest, decent, loyal, and comradely to members

of our own blood and to no-one else. What happens
to the Russians, what happens to the Czechs, is a matter

of utter indifference to me. Such good blood of our own
kind as there may be among the nations we shall acquire

for ourselves, if necessary by taking away the children
and bringing them up among us. Whether the other

peoples live in comfort or perish of hunger interests me
only in so far as we need them as slaves for our Kultur.

Whether or not 10,000 Russian women collapse from
exhaustion while digging a tank ditch interests me only

in so far as the tank ditch is completed for Germany.
We shall never be rough or heartless where it is not

necessary; that is clear. This is a glory page in our history
which has never been written and shall never be written."

144 Felix laughs at his new job
Helsinki, 15 October 1943

From being virtually apolitical I am swallowed
up to my gullet in international diplomacy!

On the 15th I fly Stockholm to Helsinki to meet
with Finnish Foreign Minister Henrik Ramsay.

He authorises me to negotiate Finland's peace
with Russia via US officials here. Of course I tell

nothing of these plans to H, but suggest he sound
out the Americans himself on conditions necessary

for German peace. I assume he will shout me
down but he listens, then, behind Hitler's back,

sends Schellenberg to Helsinki to negotiate
on his behalf. The man is an enigma to me –

full of fault-lines. He vacillates between total
deluded faith in his Führer and his megalomaniacal

plans for Europe, and on the other hand, a sensible
appraisal of how the war rips the guts out of us all.

He has a pathological, paralysing fear of letting
down his Führer and also nurtures his own hidden

hopes for leadership. Such contradictory impulses
pull and pummel him, result in his appalling health.

Schellenberg returns to Berlin with empty hands
as this particular effort has not borne fruit.

A great deal of talking yet to slow the great heavy
wheels of war, now they turn with such momentum.

145 Felix meets with Hewitt again
Stockholm, 24 October 1943

Tonight I have a surcharge of energy
which prevents sleep. I have met again,

late, with Hewitt and he spelt out
conditions under which America

may consider peace with Germany.
Detailing it like this, knowing it has

been endorsed by the US President,
makes it seem possible – and that keeps

me from sleep … Clearly the US
has the upper hand and will thrash

the Germans. From the east, Russia
breathes down the Reich's neck.

The only thing in doubt is how long
it will last. Some say six months

but I think it could stretch for another
two dire years. What matters is to

prevent the total destruction of Europe
in the interim. Hewitt says minimum

conditions are non-negotiable –
at the very least the Nazi regime

has to go. That is the starting point.
We agree there needs be clarification

of finer points in the next few weeks.
Talking with Hewitt makes it seem

achievable but when I imagine H's
reaction – I see spluttering outrage

and my hope sinks. The demands will be
anathema. I offer to fly to H direct

but decide on reflection it may well be
more prudent to write these demands.

146 Felix writes to the Reichsführer
Stockholm, 24 October 1943

"Dear Reichsführer, Below are the details of an
honourable peace to which I hope you will give

your full consideration … The gratitude of the entire
world will still be yours. I have had discussions with

an American, Mr Abram Stevens Hewitt (he is not
a Jew) … Please do not hesitate, Herr Reichsführer,

I beg of you as every day brings greater destruction.
Here are the seven points I have worked out with

Mr Hewitt: 1. Evacuation of all territories occupied
by Germany and restitution of their sovereignty.

2. Abolition of the Nazi Party; democratic elections
under American and British supervision. 3. Abolition

of Hitler's dictatorship. 4. Restitution of the 1914
frontier. 5. Reduction of German army and airforce

to a size excluding the possibility of aggression.
6. Complete control of the German armament

industry by the Americans and British. 7. Removal
of the leading Nazis and their appearance before

a court charged with war-crimes … I beg of you, Herr
Reichsführer, to seize this opportunity. Fate and

history have placed it in your hands to bring an end
to his terrible war. Yours respectfully, Felix Kersten."

147 Felix returns to Berlin
Gut Hartzwalde, December 1943

Passing through Berlin en route to Hartzwalde
to be reunited with Irm and the boys, is like

passing through one of Dante's hell realms.
The city is in the grip of winter; hunger and

bombs, fear and suspicion all dog the poor
beleaguered inhabitants. Faces are gaunt,

people scurry. The enemy within as much as
without – the Gestapo has tightened its grip

while bombs rain down. The Allies increase
their campaign and the city is already at

their mercy. These sights only make me more
determined than ever to do something

for concentration-camp victims as Günther
and I have planned. I need to discover whom

else I can count on for help – Schellenberg
and Brandt of course. But how will I convince

H to betray his Führer and ideals he has held
so close? I marshal my arguments as I ride.

148 Irmgard talks of Felix's modest success
Gut Hartzwalde, 22 December 1943

They are the strangest Christmas
presents he has ever received.

Only a 'Himmler' (twisted body,
twisted mind) could think of giving

one man's liberty to another as
a gift. He adds the following

to his growing journal tally: six
Germans, eight Dutchmen,

four Estonians, one Dane.
The need is so vast, he torments

himself with not doing enough.
I need to remind him that here

are another nineteen lives, snatched
out of the Nazis' maw.

149 Elisabeth explains that Felix is a man
who loves his food

Chancellery, January 1944

To himself he is gastronome, gourmet, but others call him
    glutton. What can I say – he loves his food!
    It takes a lot of energy to unlock bodies
    tied up tight in pretzel knots.

German cooking suits him well – Kartoffelpuffer and
    schnitzel and home-cured bratwurst
    with sauerkraut, strudel lashed with
    cream (his lips are moist), food to keep
    those winter nights at bay.
    Best of all is food from home
    like his Mutti used to make,

German with a strand of Russian thrown in.
    Gifted in the kitchen, nothing fancy,
    but what she cooked, she cooked with love.
    Rassolnik was his favourite, ever linking
    Irmgard and his Mutti in his mind.

That was before the war when plenty reigned. Then came
    rationing, coupons, food laws prohibiting
    even growers from home slaughter.
    Control of food – they said –
    was vital to the war. Clandestine was
    how the pigs and cows were killed
    at Hartzwalde and cop the risk.
    At least we ate – when most of Europe starved.

He used food to snare the Reichsführer. Like Felix,
    the Herr loves his ham – he had not eaten
    one for months. Hard to get and he
    cannot bear the taste
    when knots tie his gizzards inside out.

Felix had requested special status for the Estate –
    the Herr had refused. Each time they cut
    a creature's throat
    they risked their lives –
    the punishment for breaking
    food laws is death.

The Gestapo is on Felix's tail, wary of the sway they think
        he practises over Himmler.
        I fear for Irmgard and the boys
        alone in Hartzwalde while he serves H
        in Berlin. Sitting ducks they are –
        those thugs are looking
        for just one lapse – a breach
        of slaughter laws could be the perfect
        excuse to have his head.

One day he sneaks an illegal ham into Chancellery.
        When Himmler has surfaced from his bout,
        can bear the thought of food, Felix pulls it
        from his satchel with a flourish.
        Fat, juicy, salted just so.

He cuts them one slice, then another.
        Felix tells me how the Herr licks his lips,
        marvelling at how many coupons
        Felix must have saved!

Felix has him just where he wants him – all he has to do
        is spring the trap. "But Herr Reichsführer,"
        he says, "it is not coupons.
        This ham comes from a pig
        slaughtered at Hartzwalde!"
        Felix knows the Herr is a stickler, this
        will wrack his guilt. True to form
        Himmler throws up his hands, horrified
        to be unwitting party to a crime.

Felix makes it clear they have two choices – either they go
        together to the gallows or H grants extraterritoriality,
        permitting slaughter.
        Himmler sweats it but two days later
        Felix bursts through the apartment door, waving
        official papers in his hand.
        Himmler granted exactly what Felix had asked!

Felix played him like a dream. It is funny in a way
        but also hard to credit. A man like Himmler –
        to get so het up over that –
        a trifle he could have made to disappear,
        when all the while the blood and gore
        is streaming from his hands.

150 Felix plants a seed
Felix's apartment, Wilmersdorf, Berlin, February 1944

I do not mention anything
of the Günther plan directly

to H but the seed I plant is
this: "How noble and great

a Germanic leader would be
if he showed mercy towards

the most unfortunate victims
in the concentration camps."

I drop it into the fertile soil
of H's vanity. Enough for now.

151 Felix and Irm return to Stockholm
Stockholm, April 1944

Under the guise of returning to Stockholm *supposedly* to
assist Finnish soldiers *supposedly* convalescing there,

I cajole H into letting me leave for another two-month
stay. It is on the strictest proviso that we return to Berlin

and I resume regular treatments. He is an addict – and
I the drug master, providing or withholding drugs.

It gives me considerable sway. Irm and I drink the Capital
in – the colours, smells, absence of threat. People sit

in cafés and have loud, happy conversations without
lowering their voices and looking over their shoulders.

There are cakes and *choklad*, as much as you wish.
"We used to live like this," I say in wonder to Irm as I tuck

into a slice of *kaffebröd*. The Dutch correspondence
is in my satchel, to deposit for safe-keeping in my bank.

152 Felix rents an apartment in Stockholm

Stockholm, June 1944

Günther has been as good as his word.
Papers came through last week which

authorise me to rent the apartment
I have located. Perfect accommodation

given the housing shortage. Not palatial
and we will feel its confinement after

Hartzwalde, but so grateful to secure
somewhere to bring Irm, Elisabeth

and the boys when we make our escape.
I told Irm that we will all come together

on our next visit. Already she has installed
two of the three beds we will need for

the boys. The biggest obstacle is still H
and his desperate, clinging need of me.

153 Irmgard says "paper sheets in Sweden are better than silk sheets in Germany"

Stockholm, 6 June 1944

At last the Allies have landed
in Normandy! Announced via
the radio this morning before
we leave for Germany and home.
We are both overcome, cling

for a moment to each other.
Perhaps Germany will pull
through. Perhaps we will really
see peace in Europe again –
I do not know whether to stop

my hope in its tracks or let its
wings grow. We leave Stockholm
with lighter hearts than we have
had in years. Blessed, when
so many have not escaped with

their lives. The apartment Felix finds
is small. We shall have to farewell
our dear Hartzwalde for good, but
the freedom it buys is incalculable.
When The Herr gives consent,

we will bring the boys, Elisabeth
and more belongings, to start our
brand-new lives, desperate to see
an end to the slaughter, fear and
deprivation that engulf Europe.

6 June 1944

Operation Neptune, The Normandy landings

D-Day begins the Allied offensive in Operation Overlord. The largest seaborne invasion in history, the operation starts the assault on German-occupied Western Europe, leading to the restoration of the French Republic, and contributing to Allied victory in the war.

154 Felix returns to the fray
Hochwald, 8 June 1944

Two days after Irm and I return, just as we settle
into life at Hartzwalde again, H summons me

to Hochwald. I am always depressed by the mean
surrounds and accommodation here. He is very ill,

in a state perfectly open to persuasion. I am determined
to commence pressure in earnest for the Günther Plan.

Still in his nightshirt when I arrive, lying dejected
and afflicted on his narrow cot. I work him hard.

First I soften him up with flattery: "You are one of the
great Germanic leaders … of all time, Herr Himmler.

How can you countenance the killing of so many
of Germanic stock?" I ask, pleased to turn Nazi racial

theories against him. "Use your greatness, Reichsführer,
to free as many Danes, Dutch and Norwegians

in the camps as you can …" "Impossible," he replies,
sotto voce, shaken by the very idea. He stutters his regular

defence – that he cannot betray his Führer – then breaks
off the treatment to grab my wrists, locking his red-rimmed

unspectacled eyes onto mine, and demands to know
if I am aware of what I say. My hands reinforce the import

of my words. I press harder into his belly, give him
a taste of my will. He is breathing only in gulps now,

gripe and fear acute. "I know … but … I … cannot."
I do not let him prevaricate any longer. "You must give

me," I demand, "the Norwegian, Dutch and Danes!"
There, I have finally articulated the grand Günther Plan,

worked on since September last year. No room
for choice; my words and the power of my hands

do their persuading. "Ohh … yes … ohh … yes … but
give me time!" He manages to get out between moans.

"If Hitler learns one word of this …" he says beseechingly,
this most-feared Nazi monster reduced to a snivelling

mess. "Do not think of that," I reply, letting my fingers
return to their regular, healing work. He is soothed

back into quiescence again. As I step away, I tell him
I need an answer before my next trip to Sweden.

"Very well, very well," he replies. I leave his rooms
with a long-absent, bouncy spring in my step.

155 Felix has a rethink
Hochwald, 8 June 1944

I may have left H's rooms in an elevated mood
but the barracks are not far behind me before

I falter, find myself peering at my hands. What have
you done? I ask them. Stop, start, a few steps, stop

to look again, another few steps. I did not instruct
them, they just took over, gouged his gut, making

him moan. I actually inflicted pain! My hands
would not let him off the hook, insisted he capitulate.

What would Dr Ko think of me! What do I think
of myself? I flip between exaltation that the Günther

Plan now has a chance and fearing I am no better
than he or they. Not only have I used my

healing arts to force him do my will, but I have
caused pain deliberately to achieve my end!

I am sure it is a good end but the means I have used?
Another thought comes to me – the knot his guts

are in is caused by his psychic paralysis – should
he be true to Hitler or his conscience? The only way

he could be released was if he chose one or the other
– impossible to live in that abyss for long. Does it

stretch truth to say that my force forced him to take
a stand? If so then maybe I have not betrayed my

healing vows so radically. They never wrote the
Hippocratic Oath with circumstances like this in mind!

156 Felix hears about the attack on Hitler

Felix's apartment, Berlin, 21 July 1944

It has failed! Stauffenberg led the plot but it was
the work of many in the German Resistance who

want Hitler dead. Disillusioned in his leadership,
appalled by the regime's cruelty, they crave change.

They go for him at Wolf's Lair, his bastion. But
Hitler is as uncanny as a fox in dodging bullets –

or bombs – meant for him. Gravely disappointing
– Hitler dead would open the way for more moderate

leadership. But Der Chef, the boss, lives to see
another day. I knew about the plan from Schellenberg.

Now H tells me the Gestapo are on the warpath –
with orders to arrest 2,000! Before the day is out

hundreds are dead. I know Kaltenbrunner will be
having a field-day coordinating the bloodbath.

H is almost hysterical that his own plans against
Hitler will be revealed. Panting with fear, he feverishly

shreds the voluminous Stockholm correspondence.
All the carefully worked-out Günther plans to free

Scandinavian concentration-camp victims are cut
to ribbons before my very eyes. I could weep. I try

to plead but he is icy with terror and will not engage
in further dialogue. He orders me back to Hartzwalde.

157 Schellenberg warns Felix
Chancellery, Berlin, 1 August 1944

I send my warnings to Hartzwalde by motorcycle
courier. I just hope Felix receives them before

he sets out for Chancellery. "Watch out. Kaltenbrunner
has arranged to have you assassinated. Be extremely

prudent. The danger is imminent. In spite of all
the protection Himmler gives you, Kaltenbrunner

has decided to kill you … Don't follow your usual
route through Oranienburg … Take the other road."

158 Felix shakes for hours
Gut Hartzwalde, 1 August 1944

I am still trembling with how close
I came to death and the horror of

not knowing whom – or what – to trust.
When the message comes I am not

sure if it really is from Schellenberg
or from Kaltenbrunner pretending

to be Schellenberg! I retrieve the revolver
H has given me special authorisation

to carry. I have some sticky moments
thinking it through but decide in the end

to trust Schellenberg. I order the driver
to take the alternative Templin route.

Assassination attempts, it seems, *à la mode*
this month. Luckily I am able to protect

Irm from gleaning any of the danger
and she knows nothing of my ordeal.

159 Irmgard talks of harbouring Felix's old friend

Gut Hartzwalde, August 1944

Felix hears from mutual friends
that the Gestapo are after Mr R,
his Dutch underground friend.
He arranges a car for his wife
and him to flee to Hartzwalde.

We hide them for many months
until he can get papers in their
name. Nervous-making, to be
always on alert when visitors
arrive, despite Felix's attempts
to play down the danger. Usually

his tendency to exaggerate runs
fast in the very opposite direction!
For all the worry, it is wonderful
to have another man about the place
in Felix's absence. Good role
model for the boys, another pair

of strong arms and balance for
such a woman-filled farm. But
it also finally fulfils what the SS
have always suspected of dear
Felix – that he uses Hartzwalde
to harbour a host of Nazi enemies.

160 Felix goes to Hochwald
Hochwald, 8 September 1944

He is very ill, as I knew he would be,
and so angry it has given him

ein dicker Hals – a thick neck.
He takes out on me all his rage

at the Finn's 'defection'! I let him
yell the fury from his system, so worked

up he foams at the mouth and spittle
flies in all directions. When he is done

I set to work. Pummel, press, pause.
Pummel, press, pause. It takes a longish

while. Once agony retreats, he becomes
almost human again or as nearly so as

he is able. He asks courteously after
my trip and the health of my family.

4 September
1944

Ceasefire
agreed between
Finland and
Russia leading to
Armistice on 19
September.

161 Irmgard and the boys move to Sweden
Stockholm, 28 September 1944

We have finally made it, escaped from under
the eagle eye of The Herr. All of us here together
in the neutral capital of a war-torn world. Small
pocket of sanity, close your borders around us,
keep us safe. We were protected living on the Estate,

but Felix sees the daily monstering, fears the Nazi
edifice will soon crash down. You can be sure they
will make poor losers and he does not want
us – or himself – in any firing line. We owe everything
to Elisabeth – capable, reliable, loyal Elisabeth,

sister-like to Felix from the start. She has agreed
to stay on at Hartzwalde as manager. Frau Wacker
and the Jehovah's Witnesses will keep her company,
continue to work the land. I worry about them
with the Russians closing in but they are strong.

And Elisabeth, her sacrifice makes Sweden possible
for us – no way Himmler would have permitted our
departure had she not played hostage. We have
told her she will have a home with us in Stockholm
for life. She is our own dear one, our very own.

162 Elisabeth thinks aloud
Gut Hartzwalde, October 1944

Profoundly relieved to have left the cauldron Berlin
has become. The Nazis
have cooked up a lethal,
explosive mix and it will erupt
before too long
in a colossal conflagration.

Felix says they scrabble at the top, crazed, trying to outdo
each other, posturing before
the world. Time, he says,
for great humanitarian schemes.

By contrast the peace at Hartzwalde – so deep, so true,
cradled in nature's hand. It is unsettling
at first: birdsong, the burbling creek,
the cluck of the few remaining hens.
It should be balm but I have lost
the knack of being soothed,
and it takes me weeks
to stop jolting from sleep, heart pounding
at the slightest sound.

The farm rhythms are familiar from *Wochenende* visits
over many years. My duties
are made light by the Jehovah's Witness
women who are a joy
and teach me gratitude
in the face of worry.

163 Felix is jubilant
Gut Hartzwalde, 8 December 1944

Months in the making with Günther, I talk myself
hoarse on many occasions, perjure myself, use

the lowest kind of manipulation and pressure.
I have just now succeeded in getting H to agree

to the Günther Plan and the release of: 1,000
Dutch, Norwegian and Danish women and children,

students and policemen. 400 Belgians. 500 Polish
women. 800 Frenchwomen to go to Switzerland.

2,700 Jewish men, women and children. 7,000
Norwegians and 5,000 Danes. A total of 17,400 –

enormous numbers when I recall starting with
a single person – Rosterg's factory foreman back

in '40. Extraordinary! We will liberate them; they
will return to a family's desperate, loving arms.

164 Felix writes to Himmler
Gut Hartzwalde, 21 December 1944

"Dear Reichsführer, Thank you very much
for your letter dated December 12th … I would

like to thank you for your great consideration
and to confirm the agreement we reached on

December 8 … I am convinced that Sweden will
take all those you have agreed to release

and history will not forget your magnanimity …
I fly to Stockholm tomorrow with a lighter heart,

knowing that you will be certain to keep to what
you have agreed with me. With thanks, Felix"

Words from
the Volk,
Christmas,
1944

***Werden
praktisch, geben
einen Sarg* (Be
practical, give a
coffin)**

Berlin suffers
daily (American)
and nightly
(British) bombing
raids and
much of the
city is reduced
to rubble.
Black humour
flourishes.

January 1945

Nazi authorities
estimate around
4 million people
are evacuated
ahead of the
Russian advance.
The figure rises
to 7 million, then
8.35 million by
19 February. At
the end of January
between 40,000–
50,000 are arriving
in Berlin daily,
mostly by trains.

An eyewitness
writes: "Each
new train …
unloads a mass
of amorphous
suffering onto the
platform."

12 January

The Red Army
breaches the
German front
and advances
westward at
the rate of 40
kilometres a day.

165 Felix works with the Red Cross
Wilmersdorf, Berlin, February 1945

Originally it was 20,000, then 17,400, and
now, today, H has granted the release

of only 2,700! Grievously disappointing but
I school myself to be consoled by imagining

how the families will feel to have their loved
ones return. I have other schemes afoot –

plans since last August with Frau Direktor
Immfeld – an old patient. She works with

the International Red Cross and a group
of Swiss industrialists to free prisoners.

I am happy to put as many irons in the fire
as will fit, if it gives more prisoners a chance.

166 Wulff offers another opinion
February 1945

Kersten may have Himmler's ear,
but does he have his best interests

at heart? The man is so unbearably
self-important! *Auf dicke Hose*

– swaggering in his very fat pants.
As the war turns against the

Reich (and Hitler is fed rumours
of Himmler's involvement in the

attempted coup), Himmler breaks
down at Hohenlychen, unable to

bear being suspected of treachery
by his Führer. He takes to his bed,

totally collapsed, crying ceaselessly.
He calls Kersten to him but Kersten

takes weeks to come from Stockholm,
with long lists of prisoners he wants

released. Always his own agenda.
He pretends to care but he just

wants to make more contacts abroad,
further his many business schemes.

Nazi use of
technology

Zug (Train) I

The Deutsche
Reichsbahn
national railway
system runs
the railways on
behalf of the SS,
under Himmler.
They have been
in constant use
transporting
prisoners to
concentration
camps after 1942.

Many Jews pay for
their own forced
deportation.

***Zug* (Train) II**

Modern historians
say that the mass
transportation
provided by
the railways
facilitated the
scale of the
Final Solution.
The Deutsche
Reichsbahn made
approximately
Euro 445 million
in 2009 terms, for
mass deportations
between 1938
and 1945.
Contemporary
estimates of the
scale of the Final
Solution still
rely partly on
shipping records
of the Deutsche
Reichsbahn.

167 Felix describes developments
Felix's apartment, Wilmersdorf, Berlin, 19 February 1945

A version of the Günther Plan is coming to pass.
Folke Bernadotte of the Red Cross will be in charge

of the convoy called *The White Bus* scheme. It will
transport Scandinavians from the camps to Sweden.

Bernadotte has asked to meet directly with H
to discuss arrangements and, no doubt, assure

himself that what H has committed will indeed come
to pass. They meet in the presence of Schellenberg

and the Reichsführer confirms what he has promised:
the Scandinavian prisoners will be assembled in one camp –

Neuengamme – then released. Others also want to
help free concentration-camp prisoners – obviously

the word has finally spread about the evil perpetrated
there. My old friend Otto von Knieriem has been in touch.

He acts as intermediary for the World Jewish Congress
who also want my help. I meet with Otto, and Hillel Storch,

Swedish representative of the Congress. We are of one
mind about the need, the priorities, and join forces.

168 Felix describes the White Buses
Felix's apartment, Wilmersdorf, Berlin, 3 March 1945

I leave for Berlin representing both the World Jewish
Congress and the Swedish Government. Their goals

are one – to liberate as many from the concentration
camps, to prevent the Nazis blasting the camps apart

and killing the remaining prisoners who balance
precariously on the brink. When I arrive in Germany

the Red Cross is busy painting a hundred Swedish buses
white, with its own insignia and the blue-and-yellow flag

of Sweden. They seem like colours of hope to me,
welcome respite from the menacing swastika which

dominates the city. The buses will be a military convoy
and travel through war zones, under Colonel Björck,

accompanied by Bernadotte. But Kaltenbrunner
repeatedly puts Gestapo brakes on, thwarting

arrangements and countermanding H's explicit orders.
H desperately needs to discipline the man! I travel

to his HQ, contracting now closer to Berlin as the war
turns in the Allies' favour. No longer in the Ukraine,

nor even in Hochwald in the borders of Prussia.
Now H has his HQ at Hohenlychen, in the province

of Brandenburg, just fifteen uncomfortable miles from
Hartzwalde, that wild and natural world of my heart.

169 Himmler writes to Felix
Stockholm, 2 March 1945

"Dear Herr Kersten, you will be very pleased
to hear that I have realised the idea we once

spoke about. The release of 2,700 Jewish men,
women and children and their transport

to Switzerland by train. This accomplishment
is in line with the policy I had been pursuing

for many years before the war, before the unreasonable
attitude regarding treatment of the Jews.

Best wishes to your wife, children and yourself.
Your friend of many years (signed) H Himmler."

170 Of the 2,700: one voice
Swiss border, March 1945

We are crammed onto trains
without food or drink, frozen

beneath our rags. At journey's
end, desperate for release,

we expect death in any guise –
bullet, rope, dog, club, typhus,

starvation, gas. Instead, after
crossing the frontier, when

the cattle-truck train doors
are finally opened, light floods

in, dazing us. It takes our eyes
an aeon to adjust. Then we become

dazzled anew by the pristine
white of the Red Cross uniforms.

How far we are fallen to be
devastated by the nurses' tears.

CHAPTER VI

171 Felix continues to try
Hohenlychen HQ, Germany, 4 March 1945

My nerves are shredded and Gott knows
it takes a lot to disturb my equanimity.

But time runs out for us. Though the Allies
close in on the west and Russia on the east,

H is full of optimism when I reach Hohenlychen
to treat him, full of the false confidence

his delusion brings. Inside, he is all screwed up,
once more in spasming torment. After I relieve

him of the worst, I ask him if what I have heard
is true about the bombing of the camps.

His confirmation is virulent. "If we lose the war,"
he spits out, venomous, his eyes behind his glasses

bug-like, "our enemies must perish with us!
They shall not have the satisfaction of emerging

from our ruin as triumphant conquerors!"
It is Hitler, right down to the strings of slobber

flying from his mouth. As I have done for days
now, I repeat my arguments: the senselessness

of a large-scale slaughter. "Yours," I argue,
"could be the glory of having saved hundreds

of thousands of people," drawing a tantalising
picture of history (bait on which to hang his

vanity), thanking him for his magnanimity,
revering him as the greatest German leader,

ever. But he is steadfast in refusing to act against
his Führer. I have more luck in broaching

Kaltenbrunner's lack of cooperation. It infuriates H,
renders his normally sallow complexion crimson.

In my presence he instructs Brandt to give him
strictest orders to desist and cooperate fully

and completely with the Swedish Government
in all particulars. Now, we can only wait and see.

172 Wulff goes to Himmler
En route to Hohenlychen, 10 March 1945

Over the last year Himmler has made much
use of my charts, consulting them and me

before making big decisions. Schellenberg or
Kersten relays messages. Behind the scenes

I work with Schellenberg to influence Himmler
to depose Hitler, negotiate peace with the Allies,

release the concentration-camp prisoners.
As military pressure mounts and the Regime

totters, Himmler draws on me more and more.
The Gestapo billet me at Hartzwalde so Himmler

has ready access. Today he wants another horoscope
update and Kersten drives me to Field HQ. A fine

mist covers the countryside as we leave the Estate;
grey misery drapes the long columns of refugees

moving west. We travel, haltingly, along roads
studded with "carcasses of dead horses and make-

shift crosses inscribed with the … names of children
and old people who had frozen to death."

Kersten talks about his plans. As ever, full of himself,
he fills the small car with the sound of his self-

importance. He asks me to doctor H's horoscope
but I refuse to support him. He then pleads for my

help for his 'humanitarian' schemes, but I can't
abide his egoism. I tell him it would be falsification.

173 Felix works another angle
Hohenlychen, 10 March 1945

Driving Wulff to Hohenlychen, shocked when,
even at this late and desperate hour, he refuses

to use astrology to help put pressure on H. When
so many suffer, surely it is no time for these kinds

of scruples? We arrive just after H is informed typhus
broken out in the huge Bergen-Belsen complex

which houses 60,000. Disaster if disease takes
hold. The camp could become an infection centre,

imperilling all of Germany. I use everything
to maintain pressure on H. Lacking Herr Wulff's

niceties, I use anything, including this outbreak, as
terrible bargaining chips in the effort to avert deaths.

174 Felix talks about a momentous accord
Chancellery, 12 March 1945

H has been in an almost febrile state – his essential
weakness always revealed under pressure. We –

Brandt, Berger, Schellenberg and I – have bullied him
all week. He is terrified Hitler will discover his betrayal,

confusing statesmanship with a bodyguard's blind
obedience. But finally, by bolstering his always

needy ego, we manage to talk him through his fears.
I can hardly believe he is willing now to do as we ask.

If he can be prevailed upon to keep his word – no
guarantee available – it will save the lives of hundreds

of thousands. My knees tremble as he signs the most
remarkable document I have ever envisaged, detailing

the conditions agreed: 1. The concentration camps
will not be dynamited. 2. On the arrival of the Allies,

the white flag will be flown and the camps handed
over in an orderly manner. 3. No more Jews will be

executed and they will be treated as other prisoners.
4. Concentration camps will not be evacuated.

Prisoners are to remain and not sent on forced
marches. Sweden can send individual parcels to Jewish

prisoners. How deeply I feared he would renege.
Now, in a blink, my fears have turned to ecstasy.

Never in my life before have I been so deeply happy
as when I put my name to this document … invisible

representative of an invisible power, above all the
powers of the earth. H signs his name and adds

'Reichsführer'. Brandt signs his. I sign mine and some
unthought-out impulse makes me add: "In the name

of humanity. The higher power … humanity itself."
H sees what I have written, looks at me, astounded.

175 Elisabeth describes Berlin
Wilmersdorf, Berlin, 12 March 1945

We have come to Berlin for a few horror-filled days
    to close the apartment
    and take precious possessions
    back to Hartzwalde.

The City has become a war zone. The streets
    filled with dirty, uncouth soldiers
    trying their best for us.
    Refugees have arrived
    in avalanches of human misery.
    Fear is an ever-present foe.

As the opposing forces approach, everyone fears
    a bloodbath and the Nazis
    use boys as young as fourteen as cannon fodder –
    another reason to have
    removed the Kersten boys
    as far away from here as possible.

Himmler may have signed the agreement
    but I won't believe it until he has
    put that scrawly signature on
    the actual orders.

Words from
the Nazi
lexicon, 19
March 1945

**Hitler's
'scorched-earth
policy'**
Hitler orders
the destruction
of German
infrastructure as
the war ends to
prevent use by
Allied forces.

176 Felix fights for a city he loves
Chancellery, 14 March 1945

The essence of the Nazis is amplified
in this, their dying days. Destruction

is their hallmark – bridges, oil wells,
ammunition dumps, dams, anything

which might benefit the Allies – or the
people! Detonations shake the ground

and the air fills with choking dust.
Everything is makeshift, provisional –

buildings or structures no longer convince
of permanence. Fighting around Cologne

steps up and we anxiously await the final
breakthrough of British and US troops.

Dr Brandt reveals that Hitler has already
issued orders to smash Den Haag, that city

I love, where I made my home for so many
years. The inhabitants have not been warned

and will not be. I cannot bear the wanton
waste. Immediately I seek out H for his

confirmation. "If we are to perish," he rants,
"those Dutch parasites will perish as well!

I need to use all the big guns in my arsenal,
remind him of his debt to me, how many

times I have come to him in his direst need,
how he may not even have survived without

my constant help. "Is this the way to repay
my kindness?" I ask. Amazingly, it works!

The next day he tells me he has ordered
the Commander-in-Chief of the SS in Holland

not to start blasting until he hears the go-ahead
direct from the Reichsführer himself.

177 Himmler is apoplectic
Chancellery, March 1945

We have the most wonderful plan
to stop those Russian swine in their

tracks. Panzerjagd – our warriors,
to a man, loyal and brave, heroes

going into battle against the tanks,
cycling furiously for the Führer,

rocket launchers blazing! Traitors
say the Panzerfaust are not strong

enough to penetrate the tanks' shells!
Vile treachery. How can we win

the war with treason like this? People
caught saying this will be thrown

into cells at Prinz-Albrecht Strasse
for a dose of their finest. Being run

over by a tank repeatedly will be tame
by comparison. Our boys are miracle

workers who will win the war for
us! I will not countenance such

rubbish. It is "ein absoluter Schwindel",
an absolutely reprehensible lie.

178 Felix turns the screws
Wilmersdorf, Berlin, 17 March 1945

Despite the signing of the agreement, I greatly
fear the fate of the camp prisoners left in H's

unreliable hands. How to bring new pressure
to bear on him, to sign actual orders to camp

commandants? I have hatched a most unlikely,
audacious plan. Could I arrange a meeting

between him and a Jewish representative? Mythic,
archetypal, surely the most improbable meeting

in history! Could H be talked into seeing a real
person instead of the imagined enemy born

of his and Hitler's hate-filled delusions?
In my presence, the meeting would be in a spirit

of respect, designed to bring out what passes
for H's humanitarianism, rudimentary and in danger

of extinguishment though it is at every turn.
My treatments evoke it, and my words can be

turned to pluck the chord of his vanity. Perhaps
a face-to-face meeting may wring further, more

far-reaching concessions from him … particularly,
force him to disobey Hitler about destruction

of the camps. When I first raise the idea he is still
under the grip of Hitler's hypnotism, refuses flat-out:

"I can never receive a Jew. If the Führer were to hear
of it he would have me shot dead on the spot."

Not that he, Himmler, refuses because of his own
feeling but because he fears Hitler! I am ready

for this and act as though this is only a minor
obstacle, reminding him that as head of the SS

he can surely arrange the secret landing of our plane
in Germany, passing through borders without Hitler,

Goebbels or Bormann ever hearing of it. He grants
this is true. Single-handedly I am stage-managing

an opera of epic proportions, directing heavyweight
performers in a gala of significant import. Can I really

pull it off? I propose the talks be at Hartzwalde,
away from prying eyes, bombs and Chancellery

court intrigue. I add, it is up to him who should attend.
He readily names Schellenberg and Brandt. The finale

is asking him if I can inform Herr Storch of the World
Jewish Congress. A tense moment later he replies:

"Yes, Herr Kersten, you may." Provided I accompany
him. He then gives his word that he will personally

guarantee Storch's safety and freedom. I breathe out
a long-held breath of relief. Slowly, most precariously,

we move a step closer to achieving our goals. I depart
on March 22 for Stockholm, buoyed, bearing this news,

like some weighty olive branch, to meet with
Günther and Storch to finalise our desperate plans.

179 Felix describes his report to Günther
Stockholm, 22 March 1945

Günther is amazed at what we have
achieved, particularly the freeing

of the 2,700 prisoners with at least
20,000 more to come, many ill,

most half-starved. He reasserts Sweden's
willingness to do everything in her power

to transport and house them. "A political
event of global importance," he calls it.

But hundreds of thousands more suffer,
in direst peril and I cannot rest until

there is not a single thing more I can do
on their behalf. Günther is incredulous

that a meeting between Storch and H
could even be contemplated, let alone

possibly proceed. "If it does," he says,
"it will be an indescribable miracle."

180 Felix's small and large successes
Stockholm, 23 March 1945

I receive a letter from H today telling me
that my intervention on behalf of

former mayor of Vienna Karl Seitz has
been successful. But bigger is seeing

incredulity on Storch's face when I
pass on H's invitation to come

to Germany to have coffee with him!
He takes some considerable

persuading I have not spoken in jest –
his face crumples, as members of

his family have already perished
in the camps. Clearly thinks it a cruel

joke. I immediately reassure him but
not until he witnesses me speaking

to H in Berlin on the secure phone line
does the haunted look leave his face.

He rings the Congress in New York and
gets permission to accompany me.

181 Felix explains his frustration
Gut Hartzwalde, April 1945

H still prevaricates about whether he will
or whether he will not meet with Storch.

He is so impossibly hard to deal with!
Schellenberg says H throws his hands up,

claiming he can not possibly meet with
the Jewish representative with Kaltenbrunner

breathing down his neck, ready to report
the smallest infraction to the Führer.

Schellenberg advises H of the simple expedient
of meeting when K is known to be away.

The first British troops (11th Armoured Division) enter the Bergen-Belsen concentration camp, after securing a truce with SS guards on 12 April. When they enter the camp, the soldiers are totally unprepared for what they find. Inside are more than 60,000 emaciated and ill prisoners, in desperate need of medical attention. More than 13,000 corpses, in various stages of decomposition, lie littered around the camp.

182 Felix makes plans
Stockholm, 17 April 1945

At the last minute Storch has said
he cannot make the meeting but he

deputises Norbert Masur, Director
of the Swedish Section of the World

Jewish Congress in New York, to
come in his stead. H has apparently

taken Schellenberg's advice and
scheduled the meeting for 19 April,

when Kaltenbrunner will be away.
And so we enter the final act.

183 Felix updates his tally
Gut Hartzwalde, 19 April 1945

Thankfully the *Tausendjähriges Reich* breathes
its last, after the longest decade in history.

Dr Brandt is kind enough to keep me fully
appraised of each of the Reichsführer's acts

of clemency. In this charged period when
everyone wants to prove his name, H is no

different. Notable releases include: the last
Jehovah's Witnesses, King Leopold of Belgium,

Professor Seip, Count Arco, Count Bismarck,
Ernst Hepp, Reidar Aulie (the Norwegian

painter), Princess Jean Sapieha, Countess
Ernest Fleurieu, and Heinrich and Alexander

Bondy. H is still looking for a pardon for
Theodor Seltzer. Not an insignificant haul.

16 April 1945

The Battle of
Berlin commences
on this day and
becomes the final
offensive of the
Second World
War.

184 Felix and Masur, en route
Gut Hartzwalde, 19 April 1945

Masur and I depart Stockholm at 1400 hours, the only
passengers in one of the last aeroplanes we hope will

ever bear the swastika. We sit alongside mountains
of Red Cross parcels, forced to silence by engine racket.

Masur is young, remarkably self-contained for his years.
We arrive at Tempelhof airport towards dusk, greeted

by an SS Officer with neatly clicking heels, stern Heil
Hitler salute. Masur politely raises his hat and replies

"Good evening", equal to the occasion. We receive
Masur's safe-conduct pass and await our transport,

on edge, wondering why the vehicle is late, fearing
H has reneged. The loudspeaker crackles into life.

Goebbels addresses us, regaling the listening public
with the surreal news that while bombs drop around

them, and mortars pound their city, while food supply
grows tighter and their sons and grandsons perish,

while Russia marches from the east and Britain
and America converge from the west, he has momentous

news, bound to be of solace. "Rejoice …" he exhorts,
"tomorrow, 20th April, is the birthday of your beloved

Führer!" Masur and I are speechless with incredulity,
exchange bewildered glances. Not even out of the airport

and already we have entered the madhouse. Eventually
one of H's drivers arrives. Nerves taut, en route to

Hartzwalde, we pass through Berlin, ghost city, lit
by the all-seeing moon and flames from incendiaries

on the horizon. Our progress is hindered by huge mounds
of rubble; girders, spaghetti tangles of wires and tubes

that once were buildings. We manage to exit the city
confines before the nightly bomb avalanche.

We reach the shelter of the forest, behind us searchlights criss-cross the sky. No anti-aircraft stutters answer.

All taken to the front, the driver says. Unbearably depressing
to witness such destruction and Berlin – so undefended.

We drive beneath the meagre protection of trees and arrive
at Hartzwalde by midnight. Elisabeth greets us with candles

as the power station has been bombed. Together we wait up
for Schellenberg, due to arrive later tonight. Mostly silent,

we rest, preparing for the demands to come. The candles
glimmer in the darkness, small and frail islands of hope.

185 Felix describes the preliminaries
Gut Hartzwalde, 19 April 1945

Schellenberg arrives in civilian clothes at 0200 hours,
weary with depression at how the madmen still scuffle

and jockey for advantage so close to the end. As H's
Foreign Affairs man, he warns me that H is unwilling

to make further concessions. Bormann and others
are putting on pressure and Schellenberg adds:

"The Führer and the Reichsführer both believe
it is time as never before to be ruthless ... I'm afraid

Himmler may end by giving in and going back
on the promises he made to you." My heart sinks.

I spend the next two hours speaking as persuasively
as I know how. Though Schellenberg has been

with us, it seems now he advocates for Himmler.
I need to bring him back. I review our goals:

"We must get H to confirm what he has previously
promised, particularly the security of the Red Cross

bus convoy which has still not left German borders,
the release of prisoners, and finally, to refrain

from blowing up or evacuating prisoners from
the camps, as Hitler and his henchmen continue

to insist." I have reiterated these points so many
times my mind spins like a record on a phonograph.

Just before sunrise we retire to our rooms for a few
hours. All I want is sleep but a nervous buzz fills

my body – I cannot settle. I process conversations,
and what we have at stake. I am amazed at Masur's

maturity; outwardly calm, marshalling arguments,
keeping his mind focused on the goals. He seems

to wear his duties lightly but appearances can be deceptive.
Thoughts chase each other, endlessly driven by fears

of what could go so disastrously wrong. However I try,
I find no way this night to discipline my jumping mind.

186 Words from Felix's lexicon
Gut Hartzwalde, 19 April 1945

***Abschied* (Farewell, parting, resignation)**

Noises intrude on my attempts at rest –
forest sounds masquerade as Russian

soldiers crunching twigs underfoot,
preparing to burst through my front door.

The Red Army advances close by
so I tread another circuit of the house

checking doors and windows. I know
this is my last night at Hartzwalde

and walk in a daze through the rooms
farewelling favourite furniture, precious

artworks, children's toys. So many happy
years here, Irm and the boys present

in every room … The minutes tick by,
time never so heavy. I return to the fire

and sit with Elisabeth in tense, silent
companionship. Tomorrow, after meeting

with H, she and I leave for Stockholm
by car – the journey will be perilous

and we will have to pass through
the worst as Berlin is pummelled

and the Reich puts up a last desperate
stand. I leap ahead to journey's end

and cannot wait to feel the confining
walls of that small apartment and the

cacophony of family chaos close around
me once again. I am at the waterfall's edge.

187 Felix worries
Gut Hartzwalde, 21 April 1945

When we reconvene, Schellenberg
makes it clear he is on board again.

Relief, momentarily undammed,
courses through my tension. Over-

night, inexplicably, he has made
an about face on every issue, now

promises Masur his full unqualified
support. The house shakes from

nearby explosions, setting us further
on edge. Each time the ceiling rains

a fine powder down on us.
Schellenberg returns to Berlin

to collect the Reichsführer who has
been at the Führer's 56th birthday

party. What they find to celebrate
is hard to fathom. He will return with H

and Brandt tonight. Time hangs heavy
as a shroud, muting all, even the

detonations. Nothing of permanence
in this ripped-up, war-torn world.

188 Felix describes Himmler's arrival
Gut Hartzwalde, 21 April 1945

Long after midnight when finally his vehicle
splashes along the muddy drive. Schellenberg,

Brandt and then H clamber from the car, H
in full military regalia. Medals, including his

Iron Cross, glint on his jacket, dangle across
his narrow chest. He is straight from the party,

in the bombed-out ruins of the Reich Chancellery,
where I have treated him so many times. Sober,

despite the festivities, as the Führer cools towards
him. Even in his bunker, rumours reach Hitler

of H's actions. Their delay tonight is due to
Allied bombs; ditches provided shelter more

than once. Despite months of prevarication
H has come, as he said he would. Extraordinary;

sudden anxiety surges at all that could go wrong
in bringing these two erstwhile archetypal

enemies together. Was it madness – or worse,
hubris – to even think I could make it work?

189 Felix warns the Reichsführer
Gut Hartzwalde, 21 April 1945

Taking deep breaths I usher the others
inside, keep H a moment to remind

him that both he and Masur are my
guests. "The whole world is appalled,"

I remind him, "at Nazi treatment of political
prisoners. This meeting," I add, "is your

last chance to show that Germany is
able to be humane," though I doubt if that

really is the case. "Have no fear, dear
Dr Kersten," he reassures me, "I am here

to bury the hatchet between us and the Jews."
I never thought to hear this from his

mouth. Alongside our other business
I urge the immediate capitulation of

German troops in Norway, Denmark
and Holland, resort to all my old bullying,

cajoling tactics with him – for the last time.
He flips into an immediate frenzy, spraying

me in saliva as he struggles to contain
his vehemence: "There is no other authority

in Germany than the Führer!" I calm him
but his instability does not bode well.

190 Felix's foreboding
Gut Hartzwalde, 21 April 1945

I take him to the room where Masur is waiting
alone and introduce them. They bow slightly

in formal acknowledgement, then Schellenberg
and Brandt join us. Elisabeth serves the coffee

and cake I brought back from Stockholm –
luxuries now in Germany – and leaves us alone.

We sit in apparent peace together, but the suffering
of so many hovers in a miasma between us.

Then Himmler starts describing Nazi policy
towards the Jews – in all its guises, starting

with his Madagascar plan, trying to establish
his *bona fides*. Masur interjects politely when

he has points to make. H is dogmatic, pedantic –
never happier than with a captive audience.

We let him go on, but when he starts to justify
the concentration camps we all stiffen. He says

that they really were more like education camps
and the crematoria were necessary to deal with

all those who died of disease and epidemic.
Masur hardly contains himself at the appalling

affront, interrupts fiercely. "Crimes have been
committed in those camps." He protests, obviously

very distressed. "I concede it happened occasionally,"
H says, giving the same concession he gave me

in our debates. "I have punished the persons
responsible." He must be referring to Koch,

Commandant of Buchenwald, whom he ordered
shot for corruption and prisoner ill-treatment.

The conversation swerves dangerously, right
where it is most perilous for it to swerve.

"Let us not discuss the past," I say, forcing myself
into the heat. "We cannot alter that and we will

only create the wrong atmosphere. We are
far more concerned with discussing how

much can still be saved." This allows Masur
space to start outlining his demands. "At least

all Jews remaining in Germany must be assured
of their lives, if we want to build a bridge between

our peoples for the future," he says, eloquent
and generous even under this duress. "We must

see the release of all Jews," he concludes.
H does not respond and I can see his unease.

Even with the blade of certain defeat keen against
his throat, he struggles with acting against

the Führer or – more horrifying still to him –
Hitler discovering evidence of his betrayal.

191 Felix describes the most improbable meeting in history
Gut Hartzwalde, 21 April 1945

We enter a long, many-hour discussion
which stalls repeatedly, attempting to get H

to sign the orders for which he had previously
given promises. He gets bogged down,

bemoaning how the press treat him, even when
he released the 2,700 Jews into Switzerland.

Some hours into our deliberations, worn down
by our repeated assaults on his fortress-thinking,

he finally capitulates and agrees to the immediate
freeing of 1,000 Jewish women from Ravensbrück,

but adds: "Above all, do not put them down as Jewesses,
but as Poles." This concession seems to knock through

the door which had been so resolutely locked before us.
In addition he signs documents permitting the release

of: fifty Norwegian Jews, fifty Dutch Jews, fifty Dutch
women, one Frenchman, three Frenchwomen and

several Swedes. We reiterate that the Red Cross must be
allowed to send relief parcels to inmates of the camps.

Finally, after months on the drawing board, H agrees
to issue the actual written commands which will

ensure the camps are not dynamited, the prisoners
not annihilated. He signs orders to all Nazi death-camp

directors: not to kill their inmates as insisted by Hitler.
Gott im Himmel, he has actually done the big thing,

that act we have been planning and hoping towards for
months. Masur and I exchange an incredulous,

relieved glance. Brandt and Schellenberg assure me
that they can raise the numbers considerably.

H makes no demand for his personal future,
as I assumed he would. I contain my surprise.

192 Felix reflects
Gut Hartzwalde, 21 April 1945

Masur has finally achieved what
he came for, and what I had

hoped for has, remarkably, come
to pass. Like trying to dislodge

victims clenched in the determined
bony grip of the Grim Reaper

himself … how much coercive
force we needed to exert! Too

weary for jubilation, exhausted
satisfaction suffuses the group.

Approaching 0600 hours when
we wind things up. Dawn spreads

its softness and renewal despite
war waged on every side. A new

day arrives, a new day which takes
us all towards our fates and that

of the poor benighted country
we each, in our own ways, serve.

193 Felix describes Himmler's leave-taking
Gut Hartzwalde, 21 April 1945

Before he gets into the waiting car, Himmler takes
me aside and we pause a moment in the garden

to take in the great apocalyptic clouds of smoke
billowing over Berlin. Brandt has told us the city

is nearly encircled, and already there is heavy street
fighting. The early morning is cacophonous with artillery

fire. We know this is our farewell although neither
of us mentions it by name. "We have made grave

mistakes," H says in a low voice, almost as if he is
talking to himself, or making a death-bed confession.

"If I could begin again I should do many things differently
… What will History say of me? … Small souls and those

who hated me will see to it that everything good I
wanted to do for Germany will be interpreted

for posterity as wicked and bad." For the first time,
I find nothing to counter his monumental denial.

We shake hands. There are tears in his eyes. "Give my
greetings to your wife and children," he says, voice

choked. "I thank you from the bottom of my heart for
having helped me with your treatments for so many

years. Do not think badly of me. Help my poor family if
you can. Auf Wiedersehen." The other men now join us.

H shakes hands and repeats his farewell. Then he
and Schellenberg get into the car and drive off.

24 April 1945

Himmler makes
an offer of
surrender to the
Western Allies
alone. The offer is
turned down.

28 April

"Hitler hears a
BBC radio report
of Himmler's
peace negotiations
with Eisenhower.
According to
eyewitnesses
in the bunker,
Hitler rages like
a madman with
a ferocity never
seen before, when
informed of the
betrayal. Himmler
had been at
his side since
the beginning,
earning the fond
nickname Der
Treue Heinrich
(Faithful Heinrich)
through years
of murderous,
fanatical service
to his Führer."
Now, Hitler wants
to have him shot.

194 Elisabeth talks about not saying goodbye

En route to Stockholm, 21 April 1945

Our bags are already in the boot. After the Herr
    and the rest of the party leave
    Felix and I bundle ourselves into
    coats, grab hand-luggage and creep
    under cover of remaining night into
    the car.

They know we are going but we cannot bear
    the thought of leave-taking
    so we become
    momentary cowards. A single
    cock crows

as we depart on silent tyres
    before the farm wakes.
    Harsh, melancholy
    farewell to Hartzwalde.

195 Felix talks about leaving Hartzwalde
In transit, Gut Hartzwalde–Stockholm, 21 April 1945

The drive is a blur of disjointed, surreal impressions.
Sleep impossible as the car jolts and stutters its way

forward, inch by inch. Endless checkpoints and stops
for columns of soldiers, masses of refugees, vehicles

with higher clearance than ours. We travel on the
outskirts of fighting, sometimes closer. Aircraft rake

the ground nearby with fire. The car is shaken repeatedly
by explosions. Grotesque faces loom into sight, zoom

out of focus again. Friends? Enemies? Elisabeth sags
against the opposite window, as tired as I am. I slip into

and out of trance, so exhausted from three successive
nights without sleep and the nervous energy of getting

H to the meeting. I do not let myself think of Hartzwalde
and the people I leave behind. Or of H and his fate.

Not even any more of those poor suffering multitudes
on whose behalf I have worked. When I think at all

it is of Irmgard, the boys and the welcome they will
give me. My body slumps once more into collapse.

28 April 1945

Since Himmler
is nowhere to be
found, Hitler
orders his
personal liaison,
SS-General
Hermann
Fegelein, shot
instead. Fegelein
is already under
suspicion, for
trying to sneak
out of Berlin the
day before in
civilian clothing.
After a nominal
court-martial he
is taken up to
the Chancellery
garden above
the bunker
and summarily
executed.

29 April

Benito
Mussolini,
Hitler's longest
political ally,
is captured by
Italian partisans
while he and
his mistress
are attempting
to flee. He is
executed, hung
upside down and
thrown in the
gutter.

30 April 1945

A Soviet flag
flies over the
Reichstag ruins.
Adolf Hitler
commits suicide
by gunshot in his
Führerbunker.
His wife,
Eva Braun,
commits suicide
by cyanide.
According to
his instructions
their bodies
are set alight
in the Reich
Chancellery
garden outside
the bunker.
Records in the
Soviet archives
show that
their remains
are recovered
and interred
in successive
locations until
1970, when they
are exhumed,
cremated,
and the ashes
scattered.

1 May

The Soviet army
comandeers
Hartzwalde. Frau
Wacker, Felix's
secretary, burns
Felix's papers
then escapes just
in time. The fate
of the Jehovah's
Witnesses is not
known.

196 Wulff observes Himmler
Lübeck, 28 April 1945

Even at this eleventh hour Himmler still
thinks he can convince the Western powers

to join Germany against the Russians.
His naiveté – almost as extraordinary as his

need of Hitler's approval. Reuters publish
an account of the approach he makes to

Eisenhower and he falls to pieces imagining
Hitler's reaction. As agitated as a prisoner

facing the hangman when Schellenberg and I
meet with him for an update on his horoscope.

While I prepare, he shakes, deathly pale:
"Tell me. Tell me, what I am supposed to do,"

he shouts, histrionic, pacing. "I must take my
life; there's nothing else I can do! Tell me!"

He sucks desperately on his cigar, gnaws his
fingernails to stubs. He rants, the perfect

epitome of a broken man. How ironic for him
to demand help from me – one previously

imprisoned by the Gestapo at his behest.
I leave with his whimpers still in my ears.

197 Time of death: 11.04 pm
23 May 1945

The dentist drilled till the molar was as hollow as
the thousand-year Reich. Himmler's nostrils flare

for only a moment with the stench of bone burning.
A cave in which to hide cyanide – smaller than

the Zyklon B canisters used in the camps, but just
as lethal. Chemicals courtesy of IG Farber, Nazi

supplier. Himmler practises inserting the phial
into the gap in his lower jaw, right-hand side,

rehearses flicking the stopper with his tongue.
He imagines crushing phial between teeth.

Keen for the knack, timing himself under pressure.
Flick with his tongue, crunch with his teeth,

he imagines tasting the almost instant oblivion
he hopes will save him. After the maelstrom

at the end, his last-ditch efforts to save himself,
he flees for the Alps. Another eyepatch-disguised

wanderer sleeping rough, carried by the great
human river washing through Europe. River enough

to absorb riffraff alongside refugees. The British
nab him. Chatty, they say, but eyes … steely …

bereft of expression. They know he carries poison,
make him strip, force his mouth open, spy too late

the telltale black knob protruding. You can feel
their clutch of panic. A flurry of hands, prising.

"Quick, get him to the window for light! Get his
mouth open!" So close to cuffs, claiming him prisoner.

Himmler flicks the phial free, slams teeth together
crunching glass into shards, unconscious even before

2 May 1945

The Germans
surrender Berlin
to the Red Army

4 May

The last White
Bus transport
leaves with
rescued political
prisoners
transported
by ferry from
occupied
Copenhagen
in Denmark
to Malmö in
Sweden.

8 May

Victory in Europe
Day (V-E Day),
marking the
formal acceptance
by the Allies of
Nazi Germany's
unconditional
surrender. The
war in Europe
ends.

his gums bleed. Desperate to save him, to force him
to pay, they upend him, hold him like an awkward fish

by the tail, feet high. They pump his stomach, force
emetics; their prize catch slipping away. His end –

naked, undignified. Officers dress his corpse, arrange
limbs for photograph. His post-mortem chin pokes

feebly into space. Nothing warrants how composed
he looks; hands gathered on his gut like a Burgher.

You want death to have dishevelled him, limbs
disordered, face in rictus. You want death to break

into him, rip him apart. Instead, he summons death,
in control to the end. Sergeant Austin wraps his body

in camouflage netting, ties it with Army telephone wire –
ordinary baggage, easily disposed. The Sergeant drives

to the heath, digs a hole, dumps the body. His revenge
ensures no-one ever knows where Himmler is buried.

198 Felix muses, at the end
Stockholm, May 1945

Nothing stamps me more indelibly than
the welcome Irm and the boys give me

when Elisabeth and I arrive here after
our horror journey. No words for

my utter prostration of spirit and body.
Like so many others, I reach my doorstep

besmirched and besmeared. For my dis-ease
I prescribe my children's raucous innocence,

the clean orderliness of home, the devotion
and care of my wife. Straight-talking simplicity.

I take my own medicine. When I feel those
multiple arms fold lovingly around me (grubby

fingers never more welcome!) I know, finally
it is over – the whole bizarre, grotesque six-

year ordeal. We will rebuild our lives, my
massage practice, and Hartzwalde, most

cherished world of our hearts. This time
in Swedish countryside, land on which we –

and the children – can thrive. Now, having
learnt history's lesson of impermanence,

adapting precepts from Dr Ko, we can rebuild
our heartworld not with bricks and mortar

but with help given to others, and with our
own dearest ones at the core.

199 Felix is finally granted Swedish Citizenship

Stockholm, 1953

Eight years of semi-normal postwar life, raising
a family, rebuilding my massage practice while trying

to clear my name, become a Swedish citizen. I always
know proximity to H will tell against me, but I never

imagine such difficulty. First refused in '45 – because
the Government with whom I worked so closely

when Günther was Foreign Minister, falls. He supports
my application, acknowledges my crucial role

in the White Buses, the meeting with Himmler at the end
which let the buses through. Proven now that over

19,000 were released! Significant numbers. And
finally getting H to sign orders to the camp directors

not to dynamite as Hitler had ordered. But Günther's
report is ignored by the incoming Government. Other

malicious accusations follow, none more damaging than
Folke Bernadotte's, Vice-President of the Swedish

Red Cross. He finalises arrangements with H,
accompanies the buses to Sweden but completely

writes me out of history, his memoir claiming that he
conceived the project, executed all particulars!

Outrageous claims which fuel other accusations –
that I exaggerate my humanitarian role with H,

was actually a Nazi collaborator! Many support me.
The Dutch set up a Commission of Inquiry in 1948

headed by eminent historian Professor Posthumus.
Exhaustive research clears me of all charges – of

collaborating or financially benefiting from my

association with H. Also, it confirms I saved the lives

of thousands of all nationalities many times, at great
personal risk, as well as saving Dutch people from

deportation, Dutch art treasures from confiscation
and Dutch cities and installations from destruction.

No less than the truth. As a result I am made *Grand
Officer of the Order of Orange-Nassau*, receiving

the insignia from Prince Bernhard himself in August
1950. That helps, but even though the new Swedish

Foreign Minister receives a copy of the Dutch report,
my 1952 application for citizenship is also rejected,

fuelling more poisonous rumours. Grievously
disappointed, heartsore, after the risks I have taken

on others' behalf ... On April 29, 1953, the miscarriage
of justice regarding my activities and reputation

is debated in the Swedish *Riksdag* – by all accounts
a wild and heated session with many who are bold

in their advocacy of me. The authorities can hold out
no longer – citizenship is granted in October '53!

How I would love to have witnessed that sweet
vindication. Finally my family and I have security

to put down roots. Only now, almost a decade after
the end, does the war finally end for me, and for them.

200 Date of death: 16 April 1960

France to Felix was always Crêpes Suzette and Chevalier
	in Paris – he loved the romance of the city,
	cafés along the Seine,
	walking in the Luxembourg gardens.
	One of his darkest moments
	was when she – France herself,
	that bastion of the values and culture
	he held dear – capitulated.

And then his work to liberate French citizens
	from the camps,
	from Gestapo clutches.
	Everything in his power to have them released
	before the end.

The *Légion d'honneur* – France's finest –
	to be bestowed by the hands of de Gaulle himself
	for the many French lives he saved.
	Deeply moved to know that France
	acknowledges what he has done, honours him.

En route to receive the medal, some 200 kilometres
	north of Düsseldorf. Motoring – no longer
	a German model
	but a solid Swedish Volvo.
	Irmgard is by his side, glad for the recognition
	this medal gives her man.
	A leisurely trip, they stop at a roadside café
	for refreshments.
	Felix feels terrible tearing in his chest,
	collapses, is rushed by ambulance
	to a local hospital.

Only 62 years old but how those war years tattered
	Felix's heart,
	greyed him prematurely.
	Struggling for three days
	for breath, to keep his heart pumping.
	His life force ebbing, the past passing.
	Accompanied until the end by faithful Irm.
	Three days later he dies.

He is buried in Sweden; one of the best restitutions
    is to be acknowledged in a marked grave.
    Medicinalrådet – Medical Councillor,
    it reads. No fanfare but simple truth.

EPILOGUE

Of the saved: one voice

Europe, May 1945

Arising side by side, like fingers on a hand:
depravity and righteousness.

Some say Kersten saves 60,000, some say 800,000.
Either way the equivalent of a large city, a small

nation. Oskar Schindler frees 1,100; Raoul
Wallenberg 100,000. Others also brave enough

to risk their lives for others. Heroes all. None
so close to the source as Kersten. Daily dialogue,

indentured labour tending the Snake-Meister.
Because of him we are carried, we crawl, hobble,

walk, run from camps and prisons. Out of Gestapo
torture cells, away from police stations. Inside

Germany and out. Thousands and thousands of us
leave Nazi custody, thanks to this man. We go

on foot, crutches, soldiers' backs, on trains, carts,
buses and cars. On faith alone. We return to our

mothers, our fathers, wives and husbands, our dear
children, friends, our darlings. To homes, beds

which ache with emptiness, to commandeered hearths,
to neighbourhoods decimated, to loss and the dark

hole of absence. To guilt and the burden of survival.
Some of us perish. In ditches by the sides of roads,

huddled in rags, together for paltry warmth. Of our
injuries, malnutrition, loss of faith, disease, broken

hearts. But when we die, we die with the dignity
of free human beings. Whether we know who liberated

us or not, we know liberty before death. Many of us
will survive the war, rebuild our lives, brick by slow

brick; resume work, study, find and squander love, birth
the next generation, the next artwork. Many will offer

silent daily thanks to this person. If our prayers
were winged, the sky would throng with thank-birds.

Heinrich Himmler and Felix Kersten

Gut Hartzwalde, the family estate

Dr Felix Kersten

Felix Kersten with his wife, Irmgard, and their three sons, Ulf, Arno, and
Andreas, at their home in Hartzwalde during World War II

Author's note

This is an extraordinary story of a remarkable man. My relationship with this story commenced over 20 years ago when I found a hardback edition of *The Magic Touch* in an op shop. It was written by Joseph Kessel, was translated from the French, and told Dr Kersten's story. I paid $1, and the pencilled price is still legible on the flyleaf, despite the book otherwise falling apart. I was studying massage at the time and envisaged a massage career for myself, so I was doubly enticed.

As soon as I read the book I was astounded by the numbers of prisoners for whom Dr Kersten claimed he had secured release. It was an Oscar Schindler-like story, but Schindler had been responsible for the release of 1,100 prisoners – the numbers attributed to Dr Kersten are as high as 600,000. Why didn't we know about him? He had achieved incredible things. But he was also an ordinary human, flawed like the rest of us. I knew I wanted to retell his story, but in a fresh manner.

As life unfolded I didn't become a masseuse at all, but began writing. At first I was writing prose but then found myself drifting into poetry. I soon realised this was 'my' medium, allowing me to say the kinds of things I wanted to say. Somewhere in those early poetry-writing years I wondered if I could retell Dr Kersten's story in poetry. I made a bold start, writing a handful of poems about pivotal aspects of the story. Then I ground to a halt, not having the poetry skills to deal with the Dr Kersten's life. I abandoned the project, on what turned out to be the first occasion of many. I went on to develop my poetry-writing skills, joined writing groups, and did the hard work of sending poems out to publications and competitions, with increasing success. Life intervened with the sickness and death of two people extremely close to me. On each occasion I abandoned the project – finding both that I didn't have the necessary concentration, and that aspects of the story were just too dark for those times in my life.

Somehow, amongst all the many demands of life, the story kept insisting that it get told. Professor Julian Lester says that "[h]istory is not just facts and events. History is also a pain in the heart and we repeat history until we are able to make another's pain in the heart our own." So acutely did I experience this that I hung in for the decades it has taken to research and write this story – a 25-year odyssey.

Ethical considerations engaged me early on, including the question of who had the right to tell a Holocaust narrative. I had come to the story through massage, but did I, a Gentile, have a right to write this tale? Jewish people were not the only victims of the Nazi regime, nor were they the only people whose release was secured by Dr Kersten. But they were one group that I could contact to pose this question. My thanks to Zvi Civins, the longsighted ex-Director of Education, Jewish Holocaust Centre in Melbourne, and to the generous group of Holocaust survivors, all of whom endorsed the project, saying that it was acceptable to them for me to write Dr Felix Kersten's story.

Another challenge for me was living with the story, with all its deeply embedded horror, long enough that I could feel my own sense of where the line between dark and light fell – both in the story and in the characters. I was guided by Solzhenitsyn's famous words: "… the line dividing good and evil cuts through the heart of every human being."

I also needed to choose whether to find or give a voice to Himmler in the text. I stalled on that threshold for some years, unwilling to allow this man who had wreaked such destruction, to speak. I came to the conclusion that he needed to be there, but never inseparable from the horror of his deeds and beliefs. Then Dr Kersten's bravery and actions could take shape, bearing witness to how it might be possible to interact with someone so evil. However, I found it extremely difficult to integrate Dr Kersten's claims that the massage process 'humanised' Himmler somewhat, however momentary and incomplete this humanisation was. How to present this in the work with the correct degree of balance and weight, juxtaposed with all the wrong Himmler did? Whatever vestiges of humanity I attribute to him, none of them release Himmler from full responsibility for the horrendous deeds he enacted and caused others to enact. To my mind it is scarier and more challenging to accept the possibility that Himmler (and others like him) demonstrated rudimentary humanitarian elements, rather than being total monsters.

In researching the story, the Nazis' particular relationship with language became apparent; how they distorted and corrupted it to their own ends. Each Nazi-word represented a significant civic violence, and breach of trust by the regime; one of the main propaganda tools they employed to brainwash German citizens. I started writing pieces to capture some of this corruption. Soon I had entitled them *Words from the Nazi lexicon*. Then I added words from the lexicons of other people in the story – Dr Kersten and his wife, by way of contrast. After I had written many of these pieces, I discovered the brilliant *Nazi-Deutsch/Nazi German: An English Lexicon of the Language of the Third Reich*. This affirmed my invention of the lexicons as explicating a whole *Weltanschauung*. The authors claimed, poetically, that "[w]ords have the potential to be a small can of arsenic – they can be swallowed without being noticed, they seem to have no effect, and yet after a period of time the effect of the poison becomes apparent." This informative and horrific resource was invaluable in amplifying my construction of lexicons, as one way to contextualise Kersten's story.

This *English Lexicon* was one of a handful of pivotal reference works for this project – both primary and secondary sources. As I do not speak German – or any other European language – I decided early on that I would concentrate only on English texts. Prime among these were Kersten's own memoirs – in two different versions (*Memoirs: 1940–1945*, and Herma Briffault (ed.) & Ernest Morrwitz (trans.), *The Memoirs of Dr Felix Kersten*). In addition, I drew on John Waller's *The Devil's Doctor*, and Joseph Kessel's *The Magic Touch*. Kessel tells of sitting with Dr Kersten "for days", questioning and listening to him. Dr Kersten provided him with letters, awards, correspondence, dossiers, newspaper reports in German, Swedish, Dutch and English, which corroborated his claims. Kessel says, "[i]n spite of the undeniable proofs I had seen, I would sometimes refuse to accept certain episodes of the story. It could not be true. It was simply not possible. Kersten was neither shocked nor surprised by my doubts. He must have been used to it. He would simply produce, with a half smile, a letter, a document, a testimony, a photostat. And that incident had to be admitted, like everything else." Kessel provides few footnotes, and no indication as to whether conversations are quoted verbatim, imagined or, as is likely, a blend of the two. He implies that Dr Kersten endorsed his version of the story, although Dr Kersten died "just as" it was published.

My poetic rendering of Dr Kersten's biography is grounded on the facts as I have discovered them in these works, and multiple others, listed in the Works Consulted. My imagination of the characters and the times was helped along as well by the imaginings of others, including a handful of novels. I remain indebted to all these authors for both their scholarship and their imaginings.

Over many years I tried to make contact with Dr Kersten's family, wanting to seek their opinion of my version of their family story, and to offer them a chance to give feedback about any inaccuracies or omissions. Despite many efforts I was unsuccessful – until November 2018 when Ron Phelan, Bowen therapist, got in touch with me, totally out of the blue. His first series of SMS were sent en route to Stockholm. Was I the Anne Carson who was researching Dr Felix Kersten … ? Ron had to break contact as his plane was just about to lift off! He was travelling to Sweden to meet with Arno (second son of Dr Felix and Irmgard Kersten), to make a posthumous award to Dr Kersten, inducting him into the *2017 Massage Therapy Hall of Fame*. This chance contact led to my partner and me having the great good fortune of meeting and staying with Arno and his wife Christina in Sweden in June 2019. My thanks go to Ron for his reaching out, thereby adding another extraordinary chapter to this remarkable story.

Arno and Christina were such warm and generous hosts. My thanks and deep appreciation go to them for their hospitality over our three-day stay at their beautiful home, *Stensäter*, in rural Sweden. This is the home that Dr Kersten bought in December 1947, two years after war's end. It was intended to replace Hartzwalde, that home, and estate of industry, nourishment, retreat and succour for the Kersten family, and for Elisabeth Lüben, the Jehovah's Witnesses, and many others during the dire days of the war. Although smaller, *Stensäter* is also a haven, as well as a place of industry, with a forest, orchard and lake. Arno, like his father Felix, is a fine woodsman, and has passed these formidable skills on to his children.

I'd also like to thank Arno for reading the manuscript of *Massaging Himmler*, and endorsing my version of his family's story. He said that many elements of his childhood "came back to him", and that he was "… convinced that my father would have been greatly honoured by holding one copy of your coming book in his hand." He only had one small but meaningful request for a change – that the surname of his "dear Aunt Elisabeth" be corrected from Lübe, to Lüben. It was particularly moving to visit the local cemetery with Arno to see the graves of his mother and father, and just next to theirs, Elisabeth Lüben's. Their gravestones were brightened by the spring flowers that Christina had recently planted.

*

Massaging Himmler is some sort of marrying between fact and imagining, but it's difficult to describe exactly where the line between these two is drawn, and perhaps that's part of its magic. I have allowed myself poetic licence to fill in details of the inner and daily lives of the characters, many of their monologues and some conversations, always true to how they have lived so wholly in my imagination over all these years, and ultimately to bring them to life for the reader. The postcards are my construction, and the particular women whom they address are my imagining of who the recipients could have been. Sometimes, for reasons of poetic necessity, and without changing the essence, I have condensed quotations or slightly altered their tense or the arrangement of their words. I have also braided actual quotes with segments of imagined dialogue. All direct quotations are cited.

There are of course many versions of 'truth' and I have endeavoured to bring fidelity to my truth-telling of the story, in its historical context. One challenge was wading through voluminous Holocaust information to understand the broad historical sweep of Dr Kersten's story, and to position happenings in his life in this broader context. I am grateful to Dr Samuel Kohene for help with historical accuracy. Getting details of Dr Kersten's story correct was more difficult, as there are slightly different versions in different accounts. Needless to say – despite significant effort to get it right – any errors are mine.

Visiting Arno and Christina's home, where Dr Kersten himself had lived, also gave me a chance to check the verisimilitude of some of my imaginings. In one of the poems, I imagine Dr Kersten commissioning furniture when he married Irmgard. My vision was of beautifully crafted and decorated, heavy wooden bedroom furniture. When I was at Stensäter, Arno showed me a wooden wardrobe which was one of his father's pieces. Over 100 years old and crafted of heavy timber, it was exactly like my imagined pieces. In describing the writing of biography, Leon Edel claims "There is ... something that may, at times, appear even a little mystical."

I couldn't have written this book in isolation. The terrible dark context of Dr Kersten's story would have stalled me permanently were it not for my partner, family, friends and colleagues who sustained me over the years. A few crucial people helped me pick it up again when life intervened with the sickness and death of loved ones. Poet Sue Lockwood has been a faithful supporter, offering me critical feedback and encouragement at important moments. Alison Elliott, physiotherapist and healer, joined with me in the challenge of understanding the healing relationship between Dr Kersten and Himmler, in comprehending the mechanics of the type of healing massage Dr Kersten used, and co-witnessing the depths of dark material in the story. My late mother Helen Carson and late husband Ian Murray were both avid believers in the power of this story, and in my capacity to tell it.

I had great good fortune to work with wonderful mentors. Jordie Albiston, Melbourne poet and editor of distinction, saw my first handful of poems and gave me the confidence to tackle such a daunting project in as creative a manner as I could summon. Later she saw the first complete draft and suggested I position the history and lexicons as marginalia – perfect formatting which mirrors how the Nazi Party started in the margins and remained a radical and marginal group until the 1930s. I was also lucky enough to work with Kate Light in New York through Skype, benefiting in particular from her theatre experience. Melbourne poet and editor par excellence Alex Skovron provided crucial editorial advice and a much-valued Jewish perspective.

Deep appreciation to my publishers, Anna Blay and Louis de Vries at

Hybrid Publishers for believing in my manuscript – to Anna for her close attention to editorial detail, and for being so delightful to work with.

Finally my thanks to my partner Julian Bailey, concert pianist, for his constant loving support, informed critique of the poems and stalwart belief that the work would be published, despite repeated knock-backs. We have the delight of joining forces professionally to present and perform *Massaging Himmler* the Concert, pairing 40 poems from this sequence with the whole magnificent set of Rachmaninov Preludes Op 23.

The battle between good and evil is perennial and we have much to learn from individuals who are courageous enough to risk harm, and even death, and use whatever power they have to help others.

Anne M Carson
Melbourne, August 2019

Note from Arno Kersten, Felix's son

When you hold this book in your hand and open it, you will immediately notice that it is different from what you may have expected. It is a *poetic biography* dealing with the life of a person who found himself in a situation which he and, for that matter, no other person could have anticipated.

This extraordinary, interesting book gives you the possibility of learning about the power that a simple physiotherapist gained over one of the most powerful mass murderers known in history – Reichsführer Heinrich Himmler.

When I read the manuscript I was taken by surprise because I have never read a biography in the form of poetry. After the first few lines I got interested, and suddenly it was difficult to stop reading. I found that the book was actually about my father and I was surprised that it contained so many facts which I had long forgotten.

Then I read the book a second time and this time it was easy because it contains so much detailed information about a serious event I lived through, which has left dreadful memories for generations to come. Actually, it brought these times very much to life.

As a child I did not understand everything the adults spoke of among themselves when they came to our house to discuss with my father what was happening during the six years he was treating the Reichsführer, Heinrich Himmler. But these visits created an atmosphere of a certain tension that I came to recognise.

Anne Carson has managed to describe the six-year interplay between this mass murderer on one hand and on the other, his doctor. It is extraordinary to read her description of the way this doctor managed to get humanitarian favours from his patient, who was physically a sick person but at the same time was capable of murdering people with his pen, from his working desk.

My father was a very ordinary father with a great heart, and he sought to give assistance to those in need. He was always ready to serve people who sought help. It was a reflex and he responded without hesitation. Anne Carson's book brings out these qualities.

After the war, my father resumed his activities as a therapeutic masseur in Stockholm, and we lived a life which was completely normal and harmonious. My brothers and I attended school in Stockholm until 1948. During that year my father had not yet obtained Swedish citizenship for our family; it took another five years before it happened. My parents purchased a small farm called Stensäter, about 80 km from Stockholm, after the war. When my father was not working, and particularly during the summer holidays, we all met at Stensäter. This farm became the family refuge, a source of family happiness after the torment of the war years and the loss of all our property in Germany (the former East Germany).

Once the situation in Europe had become completely normal again, it became possible for my father to take up his previous activities in Holland and Germany. He quickly found clients; many of his old friends and patients helped him by recommending him in banking and industrial circles. He started practising in Paris in 1957 because influential people such as members of the Rothschild family, actresses like Greta Garbo and many others appreciated his talents, so his financial situation improved. My father died in Germany on 16 April 1960, en route to receive the Légion d'honneur.

I have spent my adult life sharing the story of my father's humanitarian deeds. I have written a book in French and have been involved in the making of a documentary about his life. I only became aware of Anne Carson's book in the last few months before its publication. I was amazed that she had got the details of this story – my family story – so accurate. There was only one very small correction I asked her to make – to change the name of my dear Aunt Elisabeth, whose real family name is Lüben – as she was such an important part of this story.

Arno Kersten (son of Felix)
Stockholm, March 2019

The Characters

Berger, General Gottlieb: SS General, head of Himmler's SS Main Leadership Office. He worked with Schellenberg and Kersten at the end of the war to release concentration-camp prisoners.

Bernadotte, Count Folke: Vice-President of Swedish Red Cross. He accompanied the White Buses to Sweden and later, in his memoir, wrote Kersten out of history.

Brandt, Dr Rudolf: Lawyer, Personal Administrative Officer to the Reichsführer-SS Heinrich Himmler (Persönlicher Referent vom Reichsführer SS). Patient of Dr Kersten.

Ciano, Count Gian Galeazzo: 2nd Count of Cortellazzo and Buccari. Italian Minister of Foreign Affairs and Benito Mussolini's son-in-law. Dr Kersten's patient who presented him with the Croce di Commendatore dell'Ordine di Lazzaro e Maurizio (the Order of Lazarus and Maurice) in 1940 on behalf of the King.

Diehn, August: Head of the Deutsche Kalium Syndikat (German Potassium Syndicate), colleague of August Rosterg, patient of Dr Kersten.

Dollmann, Eugen: Himmler's representative in Rome.

Goebbels, Paul Joseph: German politician and Reich Minister of Propaganda 1933–45. One of Hitler's closest associates and most devoted followers, known for his zealous orations and deeply virulent anti-Semitism, which led to him to strongly support the extermination of the Jews.

Göring, Hermann Wilhelm: German politician, military leader, and leading member of the Nazi Party (NSDAP). After helping Adolf Hitler take power in 1933, he became the second-most-powerful man in Germany. He founded the Gestapo in 1933, and later gave command of it to Heinrich Himmler.

Günther, Christian: Swedish Foreign Minister, 1939–45.

Hess, Rudolf: An original member of the Nazi Party. He joined in 1920, was involved in the 1923 failed Munich Putsch and was imprisoned alongside his leader, Adolf Hitler. Hess was devoted to Hitler and transcribed his biography, *Mein Kampf*. After prison he became Hitler's private secretary, promoted to deputy leader in 1933. In 1939 he was appointed second-in-line to Hitler as Head of State, second only to Hermann Göring.

Hewitt, Abram Stevens: Roosevelt's Special Representative in Stockholm.

Heydrich, Reinhard Tristan Eugen: SS Obergruppenführer (General) and General der Polizei, chief of the Reich Main Security Office (including the Gestapo, Kripo, and SD) and Stellvertretender Reichsprotektor (Deputy/Acting Reich-Protector) of Bohemia and Moravia (now the Czech Republic). President of Interpol and chaired the January 1942 Wannsee Conference, which formalised plans for the Final Solution. Assassinated in Czechoslovakia, 4 June 1942.

Himmler, Reichsführer Heinrich Luitpold: Head of the Schutzstaffel (SS), military commander, Chief of German Police, leading member of the Nazi Party (NSDAP) and architect of the Final Solution. Dr Felix Kersten was his personal physician during World War II.

Kaltenbrunner, Obergruppenführer Ernst: Heydrich's Deputy, replacing him as head of RSHA (Reich Main Security Office) in 1943 after Heydrich was assassinated. He was convinced Kersten was part of the English secret service, attempted to have him assassinated and had spies watch him.

Kersten, Dr Felix: Naturalised Finnish physiotherapist, masseur to Heinrich Himmler.

Kersten, Irmgard (née Neuschaffer): Married to Felix Kersten. They had three sons: Ulf, Arno and Andreas. She lived at and managed the Hartzwalde Estate from 1940.

Kivimäki, Toivo Mikael: Prime Minister of Finland 1932–36. Finnish Consul-General in Berlin.

Knieriem, Otto von: Dresdner Bank, Stockholm, friend of Dr Kersten.

Ko, Dr: One of the first Tibetan monks in the West, practitioner of Chinese and Tibetan healing methods, graduate of London Medical College. Dr Kersten's teacher.

Ley, Robert: Nazi politician and head of the German Labour Front, renowned for drunkenness and abuse of power, conspicuous even by Nazi standards.

Lüben, Elisabeth: Youngest daughter of the Lüben family with whom Dr Kersten boarded when learning massage from approximately 1925. Then his personal assistant, managing his personal affairs in Berlin and The Hague and his massage practice.

Masur, Norbert: Sweden's representative of the World Jewish Congress. He attended the meeting which pressured Himmler to release prisoners and to give orders not to blow up the concentration camps at the end of the war.

Müller, Heinrich: Chief of the Gestapo, who was involved in the planning and execution of the Holocaust.

Ramsay, Henryk: Finnish Foreign Minister, 1943–44.

Ribbentrop, Joachim von: Foreign Minister of Nazi Germany from 1938 until 1945.

Rosterg, August: Powerful German industrialist before the war, owner of mines and potassium works. Patient of Dr Kersten.

Schellenberg, General Walter: Chief Officer of Information of SS, friend of and collaborator with Kersten. His testimony at Nuremberg did much to vindicate Kersten's claims.

Storch, Hillel: World Jewish Congress representative 1940–44.

Wacker, Frau: Dr Kersten's secretary.

Wulff, Wilhelm: German astrologer. Formed an astrology group based on Aryan supremacy, became Himmler's astrologer and is said to have made accurate predictions.

Dr Felix Kersten's patient list (excerpt)

Berger, General Gottlieb: SS General, head of Himmler's SS Main Leadership Office.

Bosch, Geheimrat Dr Carl: German chemist, engineer and Nobel Laureate in chemistry. Founder of IG Farben, at one time the world's largest chemical company. The Monowitz concentration camp was established in 1942 at IG Farben's request to provide them with slave labour.

Brandt, Dr Rudolf (Rudi): Secretary to Heinrich Himmler, friend of Dr Kersten.

Buffarini, Guido: Minister of the Interior, Italy.

Cerutti, Vittorio and Signora Cerutti: Italian Ambassador to Germany and France, and his wife.

Ciano, Count Galeazzo, 2nd Count of Cortellazzo and Buccari: Italian Minister of Foreign Affairs and Benito Mussolini's son-in-law. In early 1944 he was shot by firing squad at the behest of his father-in-law, Mussolini, under pressure from Nazi Germany.

Diehn, Dr August: Head of the German Potassium Syndicate, colleague of August Rosterg. Duke of Spoleto, Prince Aimone of Savoy-Aosta, Duke of Aosta. A prince of Italy's reigning House of Savoy and an officer of the Royal Italian Navy.

Flick, Dr Friedrich: Financier, member of Nazi Party and Reichstag, steel magnate who also owned part of IG Farben. He put up most of the money for purchase of *Beobachter* newspaper by Nazi Party.

Garbo, Greta: Actor and celebrity.

Graffman, Herr and Frau: Dutch patients.

Henry, Prince: Consort to Queen Wilhelmina of the Netherlands.

Hess, Rudolf: Secretary-General to Nazi Party.

Hewitt, Abram Stevens: Roosevelt's Special Representative in Stockholm.

Hochberg-Krucz-Goray, Reichsgraf Wilhelm von: State secretary.

Immfeld, Frau Direktor: of St Gallen. With International Red Cross and Swiss industrialists, contacted Dr Kersten for his help in liberating prisoners.

Keppler, Gruppenführer Georg: SS Officer.

Kessel, Joseph: Author of *The Magic Touch*.

Langbehn, Dr Carl: Friend of Himmler's. Lawyer who first handled the case of the seven Swedish directors of Svenska Tändsticks (Swedish Match Trust) corporation.

Ley, Dr Robert: Leader of the Deutschen Arbeitsfront, the so-called National Socialist Labour Union.

Mecklenburg, Duke Adolf Friedrich von: A German explorer in Africa, a colonial politician, the elected Duke of the United Baltic Duchy and the first president of the National Olympic Committee of Germany (1949–51).

Michael I of Romania: King of Romania.

Ribbentrop, Ulrich Friedrich Wilhelm Joachim von: Foreign Minister of the Third Reich.

Rosterg, August: One of the most powerful industrialists in Germany before the war, owner of mines and potassium works.

Rothschild family: Wealthy banking family descended from a Jewish member of Court in the 1760s.

Schellenberg, General Walter: Chief Officer of Information in the SS, friend of Dr Kersten.

van Nagell, Baron E.: Dutch Ambassador in Stockholm

Wenzel-Teutschenthal, Oberamtmann Carl: The biggest landowner (and agricultural contractor) in Germany during the 1940s. He was executed at Plötzensee Prison in Berlin following the 20 July 1944 plot to assassinate Adolf Hitler.

Dr Felix Kersten's Honours

1928: Hofarts (Physician to the Queen) Koningin Wilhelmina der Nederlanden.

1939–45: Over the six years of their association, Himmler sought to bestow various honours on Dr Kersten but Dr Kersten did not wish to receive them and was ingenious about avoiding them. They were:

> Colonel in SS
> General in Waffen SS
> The Collar of the Ritter Kreuz for War Services
> German Professor of Medicine.

1940: Croce di Commendatore dell'Ordine di Lazzaro e Maurizio (the Order of Lazarus and Maurice): Awarded on behalf of the Italian King for distinguished contributions to Italian life.

1941: Lääkintöneuvos (Councillor of Medicine) is the highest Finnish ranking which a doctor can obtain. Dr Kersten was awarded this for exceptional services to Finland in 1939 and 1940 during the war with Russia. It was given by the President of the Republic and ratified by Legislative Assembly. Before Dr Kersten received the award it had only been granted four times in the history of Finland.

1942: The Cross of Commander of the Order of the White Rose of Finland.

1946: Cross of Honour of the Dutch Red Cross.

1946: Silver Medal of Merit of the Red Cross from Switzerland, Holland and Finland.

1950: Grand Officer of the Order of Orange-Nassau for interventions during the war, which saved Dutch lives, interests, property and treasures.

1950s: Nominations for Nobel Peace Prize: nine times between 1951 and 1959.

1960: France's Légion d'Honneur: was to be awarded by President Charles de Gaulle in recognition of Kersten having secured the release of a considerable number of French people during the War. Kersten and his wife were en route to receive this prize when he had a heart attack and died three days later.

Glossary

German

abwandern: to make go; euphemistic and derogatory for 'to deport'

Anschluss: lit. union; annexation by Germany of Austria

Auf Wiedersehen: goodbye

ausgezeichnet: excellent

Blitzkrieg: lightning war

Bruder: brother

danke, danke schön: thank you, thank you very much

Dankesbrief: thank-you card or letter

Endlösung der Judenfrage: Final Solution of the Jewish Question

Fräulein: Miss

Freunde: friends

gross: big

gut: good

Hartzwalde: the Kersten family estate in the former East Germany. 'Heartworld' (play on *Herzwelt*)

in der Welt: in the world

Kinder: children

Kirche: church

Küche: kitchen

Kuchen: cakes

Milch: milk

mit den besten Wünschen: with best wishes

Mutter (Mutti): mother (mummy)

natürlich: naturally

nein danke: no thanks

Oberst: colonel

Reichstag: Parliament

Schokolade: chocolate

Sonderzug: special train

Strassen: streets

Tausendjähriges Reich: Thousand-year Reich

Teppichbeisser: carpet-biter

Vater (Vati): father (daddy)

verboten: forbidden

Volk: people

Völkischer Beobachter: the newspaper of the National Socialist German Workers' Party

Wehrmacht: Third Reich's army, navy and airforce

Weltanschauung: world view

wirklich: really

Wochenende: weekend

wunderbar: wonderful

Zeitung: newspaper

Zufriedenheit: satisfaction

Tibetan

bardo of dharmata: the period of time, in Tibetan metaphysics, after death before the body begins to decay

Bodhicitta: spontaneous wish to attain enlightenment motivated by great compassion for all sentient beings

Bodhisattva: an enlightened being

Buddha: Gautama Buddha, also known as Siddhartha Gautama, Shakyamuni, or simply the Buddha, was a sage on whose teachings Buddhism was founded

Dorje: a representation of a thunderbolt symbolising the male aspect of the spirit and held during invocations and prayers.

Gompa: Buddhist institution of learning and/or mediation

malas: beads (similar to rosary) used in meditation

momos: Tibetan dumplings

Om Mani Peme Hung: six-syllable Buddhist mantra repeated as a means of transforming the consciousness of the practitioner

phowa: special prayers and chants for the death process

Rinpoche: Master, precious one

Sangha: A community that joins and lives together. Also a Buddhist monastic order

suona horn: Chinese double-reeded horn

sutra: literary precept, teaching

thugdham: state of consciousness after death before the body begins to decay – mediation masters are said to rest here for many days

Varja: Sanskrit word for Dorje (above)

Swedish

choklad: chocolate

kaffebröd: coffee cake

Riksdag: Swedish Parliament

Svenska Tändsticks AB: Swedish Matchstick Company

Works Consulted

Bibliography

Allen, Martin. *Himmler's Secret War: The Covert Peace Negotiations of Heinrich Himmler*. New York, USA: Caroll & Graf Publishers, 2005.

Baker, Nicholas. *Human Smoke*. London, UK: Simon and Schuster, 2008.

Bar-On, Dan. *Legacy of Silence: Encounters with Children of the Third Reich*. Cambridge, Massachusetts: First Harvard University Press, 1991.

Beevor, Antony. *Berlin: The Downfall 1945*. Camberwell, Australia: Penguin, 2003.

Bernadotte, Count Folke. *Last Days of the Reich*. London, UK: Frontline Books, 2009.

Binet, Laurent (trans. Sam Taylor). *HHhH*. London, UK: Harvill Secker, 2012.

Briffault, Herma (ed.) & Morwitz, Ernest (trans.). *The Memoirs of Doctor Felix Kersten*. New York, USA: Doubleday & Co., 1947.

Durham, Robert B. *False Flags, Covert Operations, & Propaganda*, retrieved 16/7/19. www.googlebooks

Furst, Alan. *The Polish Officer*. London, UK: Phoenix, 2005.

Haslam, Alexander, Reicher, Steve D. and Platow, Michael J. *The New Psychology of Leadership: Identity, Influence and Power*. Psychology Press, 2013 on www.google books.com.au

Hassel, Sven. *Reign of Hell*. Cassell Military Paperbacks, 2010, retrieved 14/7/15. www.googlebooks.com.au

Himmler, Katrin (trans. Michael Mitchell). *The Himmler Brothers, A German Family History*. Pan Books, on Kindle, 2008.

Kersten, Arno and Amara, Emmanuel. *Felix Kersten: Le Dernier des Justes (The Last of the Just)*. Paris, France: Patrick Robin Editions, 2006.

Kersten, Felix (trans. Constantine Fitzgibbon & James Oliver). *The Kersten Memoirs 1940–1945*. London, UK: Hutchinson, 1956.

Kessel, Joseph (trans. Denise Folliot). *The Magic Touch*. London, UK: Rupert Hart-Davis, 1961.

Knopp Guido (trans. Angus McGeoch). *Hitler's Henchmen*. Stroud, UK: Sutton Publishing, 2001.

Knopp Guido (trans. Angus McGeoch). *The SS: A Warning from History*. Stroud, UK: The History Press, 2008.

Kovel, Joel. "Poetry after the Holocaust", in *Dialectical Anthropology*, vol. 24, no. 3-4, retrieved 16/7/19. https://www.jstor.org/stable/29790607

Lebert, Norbert and Lebert, Stephan (trans. Julian Evans). *My Father's Keeper: Children of Nazi Leaders – an Intimate History of Damage and Denial*. Munich, Germany: Karl Blessing Verlag, 2000.

Lindsey, Kiera. "Deliberate Freedom: Using Speculation and Imagination in Biography", *Text*, no. 50 (October 2018): 2, retrieved 16/7/19. http://www.textjournal.com.au/speciss/issue50/content.htm

Longerich, Peter. *Heinrich Himmler: A Life*. New York, USA: Oxford University Press, 2012, retrieved 16/7/19. http://www.revolvy.com

Manvell R. & Fraenkel H. *Heinrich Himmler: The Sinister Life of the Head of the SS and Gestapo*. London UK: Greenhill Books, 2007.

Michael, Robert & Doerr, Karin. *Nazi-Deutsch/Nazi German: An English Lexicon of the Language of the Third Reich*, eBook. USA: Greenwood Press, 2002.

Michaels, Ann. *Fugitive Pieces*. London, UK: Bloomsbury, 1997.

Monk Kidd, Sue. *The Invention of Wings*. USA: Viking, 2014.

Morgan, J. *Gods and Devils*. Australia: JJ&C, 2014.

Rosenbaum, R. *Explaining Hitler: The Search for the Origins of His Evil*. New York, USA: First HarperPerennial, 1999.

Schellenberg, Walter. *The Labyrinth: Memoirs of Walter Schellenberg, Hitler's Chief of Intelligence*. Cambridge, Massachusetts: Da Capo Press, 1956.

Sereny Gita. *The Healing Wound: Experiences and Reflections, Germany, 1938–2001*. New York, USA: W.W. Norton & Company, 2001.

Sichrovsky, Peter (trans. Jean Steinberg). *Born Guilty: Children of Nazi Families*. New York, USA: Basic Books, Inc., 1988.

Sogyal Rinpoche. *The Tibetan Book of Living and Dying*. London, UK: Rigpa Fellowhip, 1992.

Thomas, David. *Ostland*. London, UK: Quercus, 2013.

Waite, Robert G.L. *The Psychopathic God*. New York: Da Capo Press, 1993.

Waller John H. *The Devil's Doctor: Felix Kersten and the Secret Plot to Turn Himmler Against Hitler*. New York, USA: John Wiley & Sons, Inc., 2002.

Wiesel, Elie, quoted on "Rescue", Yad Vashem. The World Holocaust Remembrance Centre, retrieved 8/7/19. https://www.yadvashem.org/holocaust/about/rescue.html

Wulff, Wilhelm. *Zodiac and Swastika: How Astrology Guided Hitler's Germany*. New York, USA: Coward, McCann & Geoghegan, Inc., 1973.

Filmography

Amara, Emmanuel. *Himmler's Doctor: A film by Emmanuel Amara*. Java Films, France, 2007.

Kosiken, Arto. *Kuka Oli Felix Kersten?* [Who Was Felix Kersten?], Mandart Entertainment Ltd, Finland, 1998.

Websites

Alpha History, "The Great Depression in Germany", retrieved 17/7/19. https://alphahistory.com/weimarrepublic/great-depression

Commentary Magazine, "The Strange Case of Himmler's Doctor Felix Kersten and Count Bernadotte", retrieved 16/7/19. https://www. commentarymagazine.com/articles/the-strange-case-of-himmlers-doctorfelix-kersten-and-count-bernadotte

Facing History, "Himmler Speech in Posen (Poland) in October 4, 1943", retrieved 16/7/19. https://www.facinghistory.org/holocaust-human-behavior/himmler-speech-posen-1943

Harbour of Hope, "TheWhiteBuses.pdf", http://harbourofhope.com/wp-content/uploads/2012/06/HoHTheWhiteBuses.pdf

History in an Hour, "Rudolph Hess and his Flight to Scotland: A Summary", Rupert Colley, 10/5/11, retrieved 16/7/19. https://www.fmhac.org/uploads/1/2/3/9/123913996/krelsteinunusualcases.pdf

In The Past Lane, "Broadcasting Extremism: The Rise of Fr Coughlin", retrieved 16/7/19. http://inthepastlane.com/fr-coughlin-takes-to-the-airwaves-this-week-sept-30-2012

Jewish Virtual Library, "The Holocaust: Timeline of Jewish Persecution 1932–1945", retrieved 16/7/19. https://www.jewishvirtuallibrary.org/timeline-of-jewish-persecution-in-the-holocaust

JStor, "Dialectical Anthropology: Poetry and Ethics After the Holocaust", vol. 24, no. 3-4, "Poetry After the Holocaust", Joel Kovel, retrieved 16/7/19. https://www.jstor.org/stable/i29790604

New York Times, "The Final Days", a review of The Fall of Britain by Antony Beevor, 8/9/02, retrieved 17/7/19. https://www.nytimes.com/2002/09/08/books/the-final-days.html?searchResultPosition=4

Spiegel Online, "Did You Hear the One About Hitler?", retrieved 17/6/19. https://www.spiegel.de/international/new-book-on-nazi-era-humor-did-you-hear-the-one-about-hitler-a-434399.html

The History Place, "The Defeat of Hitler", http://www.historyplace.com/worldwar2/defeat/downfall-hitler.htm; "The Gestapo is Born", http://www.historyplace.com/worldwar2/triumph/tr-gestapo.htm; "Reichstag Fire", https://www.history.com/topics/germany/reichstag-fire and "Triumph of the Will", http://www.historyplace.com/worldwar2/triumph/tr-will.htm

The Holocaust Explained, The Weiner Library for the Study of the Holocaust and Genocide. "Chelmno" https://www.theholocaustexplained.org/the-final-solution/the-death-camps/chelmno

uBiome, "100 Years Later: The Lone German Soldier Whose Poop Fights On", retrieved 16/7/19. https://ubiome.com/blog/post/100-years-later-lone-german-soldier-whose-poop-fights

United States Holocaust Memorial Museum (USHMM), Holocaust Encyclopedia, "The July 20, 1944 Attempt to Assassinate Adolf Hitler", 25/4/2017, retrieved 16/7/19. https://encyclopedia.ushmm.org/content/en/article/the-july-20-1944-plot-to-assassinate-adolf-hitler

Wall Street Journal, "'Hitler's Pawn' Review: Who Was Herschel Grynszpan?" 8/2/19, Ian Brunskill, retrieved 16/7/19. https://www.wsj.com/articles/hitlers-pawn-review-who-was-herschel-grynszpan-11549639436

Web Archive, Way Back Machine, "Train of Commemoration Report, Train of Memory", November 2009, retrieved 16/7/19. http://www.zug-der-erinnerung.eu/download/gutachten/Gutachten_Vorwort_DE.pdf

Yad Vashem, "Rescue", retrieved 16/7/19. https://www.yadvashem.org/holocaust/about/rescue.html

Endnotes

Dedication page

"See with … seeing hand", Felix Kersten, *The Kersten Memoirs 1940–1945*, 312.

"The world today … war years", Herma Briffault (ed.) and Ernest Morwitz (trans.), *The Memoirs of Doctor Felix Kersten*, 1.

"And so we … remember them", Elie Wiesel, quoted on "Rescue", Yad Vashem, The World Holocaust Remembrance Centre, retrieved 8/7/19. https://www.yadvashem.org/holocaust/about/rescue.html

Chapter I

7   *Blut und Boden*, R. Michael and K. Doerr, Nazi-Deutsch/Nazi German, *An English Lexicon of the Language of the Third Reich*, 1495 of 5434.

        "… fleshy … surgery", Joseph Kessel, *The Magic Touch*, 23.

8   The name of the tobacco, *Antisemit*, Michael, loc. 1105 of 5434.

9   Episode from Kosiken, A. *Kuka Oli Felix Kersten?* [Who Was Felix Kersten?].

10   "Metaphor … blood", Michael, loc. 1200 of 5434.

11   "I have waited … years", attributed to Dr Ko, Kessel, 28.

19   Detail of diamond, ibid., 25.

20   Detail of Dr Ko's prophecy, ibid., 28.

25   Detail of award confirmed in personal email, Arno Kersten, 18/7/19.

28   "Doktor … slip", Kessel, 34.

29   "Joseph Goebbels … ecstasy", Nicholas Baker, *Human Smoke*, 28-9.

31   "As anxiety … resurface", Irene Guenther, "The Great Depression in Germany" on *Alpha History*, retrieved 17/7/19. https://alphahistory. com/weimarrepublic/great-depression

35   "Göring immediately … for help", "The Reichstag Burns" on *The History Place*, 1996, retrieved 16/7/19. http://www.historyplace.com/worldwar2/riseofhitler/burns.htm

37   "What does … to walk", David Crossland, "Did You Hear the One About Hitler?" on Spiegel Online, 30/8/2006, retrieved 16/7/19. https://www.spiegel.de/international/new-book-on-nazi-era-humor-did-you-hear-the-one-about-hitler-a-434399.html

Chapter II

43   "forcing … clubs", Michael, loc. 4524 of 5434.

44   "Highest … meetings", Michael, loc. 3551 of 5434.

45   "On a swastika-bedecked … hissed", Baker, 37.

46   *Wenn der Jude*, Michael, loc. 5060 of 5434.

47   "we did not … did then", "Himmler Speech in Posen (Poland) in October 4, 1943", on *Facing History*, retrieved 16/7/19. https://www.facinghistory.org/holocaust-human-behavior/himmler-speech-posen-1943

47   *The Law … 'useless eaters'*", "The Holocaust: Timeline of Jewish Persecution 1932–1945", on *Jewish Virtual Library*, 1933, July 14, retrieved 16/7/19. https://www.jewishvirtuallibrary.org/timeline-of-jewish-persecution-in-the-holocaust

50   "[Hitler's] virtuoso truncheon", Baker, 180.

50   "We want our Führer!", "look up … truth itself", "Triumph of the Will", *The History Place*, retrieved 17/7/19. http://www.historyplace.com/worldwar2/triumph/tr-will.htm

53   This description of Felix's first meeting with Irmgard, Kessel, 37.

53   Information on the priest Fr Charles E Coghlin's radio support of boycotts, *In the Past*, retrieved 16/7/19. http://inthepastlane.com/fr-coughlin-takes-to-the-airwaves-this-week-sept-30-2012

57   Detail of Felix assisting in delivery, Kessel, 38.

60   The information about "Jews For Sale", Baker, 89.

61   "… are beaten … their blood", ibid., Zindel Grynszpan, 95.

61   "I must … protest", Ian Brookskill, "'Hitler's Pawn' Review: Who Was Herschel Grynszpan?", *Wall Street Journal*, 8/2/19, retrieved 16/7/19. https://www.wsj.com/articles/hitlers-pawn-review-who-was-herschel-grynszpan-11549639436

62   "… called *Crystal Night* … anti-Semitism", Baker, 99.

        "Pull back the Police … people", "The Gestapo is Born", retrieved
        4/9/19. http://www.historyplace.com/worldwar2/triumph/tr-gestapo.htm

64   "Most of the … amputated", ibid., 111.

64   "The best political … fear", S. Hassel, *Reign of Hell*, retrieved
        14/7/15. https://bit.ly/2jTQUJ4

65   Gudrun 'Puppi' Himmler died in 2018. Through her life she remained
        a staunch defender of her father's name and a supporter of old Nazis.

66   "… repeated near … soldering iron", "The Gestapo is Born", retrieved
        16/7/19 on *The History Place*, http://www.historyplace.com/worldwar2/
        triumph/tr-gestapo.htm

66   "They are sowing … will reap!", Briffault, 99.

69   "Doktor … Colonel!", Kessel, 51, "Holland … clientele", ibid.

70   "German troops … appearance", R. B. Durham, *False Flags, Covert
        Operations, & Propaganda*, retrieved 16/7/19. https://bit.ly/2jYeW5T,
        133-4.

72   "The smell … cordite", Alan Furst, *The Polish Officer*, 196.

72   "Look, Herr Kersten … our SS", Kersten, 79.

74   "Poor creatures … dead eyes … No, Herr Kersten … come to them."
        Attributed to Himmler, Kersten, 117.

77   The idea for *Heldisch*, Michael, ibid., loc. 2609 of 5434.

77   "… the world … purified by war", attributed to Himmler, Kessel, ibid.,
        56.

78   Kersten is awarded the Lääkintöneuvos (Finnish Councillor of
        Medicine) for this assistance.

Chapter III

83   "… sister country … enslaved her", attributed to Himmler by Kessel,
        64.

85   Detail of Kersten treating Ribbentrop and other high-ranking Nazis,
        John H. Waller, *The Devil's Doctor: Felix Kersten and the Secret Plot
        to Turn Himmler Against Hitler*, 14-18.

87   Details of visit to Kivimäki, Briffault, 20-1.

89   Details of Kersten's arguments against anti-Semitism, Kersten, 33-7.

90   "Once Christianity … humanity!", Kessel, 72, and Roger Manvell &
      Heinrich Fraenkel, *Heinrich Himmler: The Sinister Life of the Head of
      the SS and Gestapo*, 177.

91   Details of Kersten's treatment of Brandt, Kessel, 69.

92   The idea of France as a "great light", ibid., 73.

94   "It is a principle … pay for them!", ibid., 77.

94   Details of Kersten exchanging his fee for a person's freedom for the
      first time, ibid., 77.

95   "As it is … I agree", ibid.

98   Details of Kersten's underground contact, Mr R, Briffault, 29.

99   "the one inviolable … Germany", Kessel, 80.

100   Definition of *Õlsardinenmanier*, and "The first … latter's feet",
      Michael, loc. 3605 of 5434.

100   Details of the argument Kersten used to manipulate Himmler into
      freeing prisoners, Kessel, 87-8.

102   "… long cry of distress", ibid., 87.

102   "My dear … heal me", attributed to Himmler, ibid., 87-8.

104   Details of those released, Briffault, 21-6.

104   "sympathising with swine", ibid., 28.

106   This incident of Heydrich's revenge, Kessel, 91.

108   There's dispute about whether it was entire population or just
      3,000,000 first then the rest. John H. Waller, says 8.5 million but
      3,000,000 first, *The Devil's Doctor: Felix Kersten and the Secret Plot
      to Turn Himmler Against Hitler*, 20.

112   Details of Elisabeth's support of Kersten and quotes from Kessel, 106.

113   Details of conversation about Dutch resettlement, ibid., 107-19.
      Waller also deals with the purported resettlement plan, Chapter 2.

115   Kersten recounts picking the posy in Briffault, 92. After exhaustive
      postwar investigations into Kersten's contributions, the Netherlands
      Government awards him the coveted Order of Orange-Nassau,
      Waller, 22.

117   "Churchill … prisoner)", "Rudolph Hess and his Flight to Scotland
      – A Summary", on *History in an Hour*, 10/5/11, retrieved 3/10/12.
      https://www.fmhac.org/uploads/1/2/3/9/123913996/krelsteinunusualcases.
      pdf

118   "You are free … meet again", Kessel, 124-5.

120   "Frost singes … snap off", David Thomas, 255.

120   The detail of the white flannel nightshirt, Kessel, 126.

122   "… ration of … of Jews", Michael, loc. 4410 of 5434.

122   The estimate of alcohol per person, Thomas, 217. This episode recounted in Thomas, 287.

122   "The realisation … precision and detail", ibid., 224.

124   "… everything that … affects your nerves" and "The tragedy of … trample corpses", Kessel, 127. Other quotes from Kersten, 119-20.

124   The name *Pharaonengräber* from Michael, loc. 3721 of 5434.

Chapter IV

127   The propaganda potential of using the word *Parasit*, Michael, loc. 3688 of 5434.

129   Definition of *Seelenbelastung*, ibid., loc. 4309 of 5434.

129   Detail of Himmler's gift card index, Kersten, 122-3.

130   Details of Chelmno, "Chelmno", retrieved 16/7/19. https://www.theholocaustexplained.org/the-final-solution/the-death-camps/chelmno

130   Definition of *Miefmobil*, Michael, loc. 3343 of 5434.

130   Theodor Morell, Hitler's doctor, prescribed a protoprobiotic called Mutaflor. The preparation contained *E. coli* from a stool sample from a WWI German soldier. "uBiome" 10/2/17, retrieved 16/7/19. https://ubiome.com/blog/post/100-years-later-lone-german-soldier-whose-poop-fights/

132   Detail of Jehovah's Witness women being released to labour at Hartzwalde, Briffault, 113-16.

133   Definition of *Schmuckstücke*, Michael, loc. 4224 of 5434.

134   Definition of *Rosengarten*, Michael, loc. 4115 of 5434.

135   This conversation between Kersten and Himmler, and "I admit … on occasion", attributed to Himmler, Kersten, Briffault, 116.

135   "… subhumans … forgets it", Michael, loc. 4716 of 5434.

137   Schellenberg makes it clear later that Kersten did not take part in German Intelligence activities in the "accepted meaning of the term", Waller, 58.

141   Conversation "If an SS … murderer of them all!", attributed to Kersten and Himmler, Kessel, 139.

142   "Don't talk … overcome us!", Kersten, 141.

142   Details of Finland ordered to hand over Jewish population to the Nazis, ibid.

143   Detail of Dutch Prime Minister Colijn's release, Briffault, 118.

146   This conversation, "What you have … achievements only", attributed to Himmler, Kersten, 151.

149   "The peasants … for the Reich", Kessel, 150.

150   "The real … evil", Guido Knopp, *Hitler's Henchmen*, 62.

151   Details of the "House of Poor Nourishment" from Peter Longerich, *Heinrich Himmler: A Life*. New York, USA: Oxford University Press, 2012, retrieved 16/7/19, 344. https://bit.ly/2kE6LvF

152   Episode of Himmler's teasing of Kersten, Kersten, 158.

153   Details of episode and "But how stubborn … Eh, Kersten?" attributed to Himmler, Kersten, 170.

154   "pompous … ostentatious elegance … ambitious", Wilhelm Wulff. *Zodiac and Swastika: How Astrology Guided Hitler's Germany*, 79-80.

157   Numbers released from Kersten, 128.

158   Details of this episode regarding Hitler's health, ibid., 165-6.

159   Details of this conversation between Himmler and Kersten regarding Hitler's health, ibid., 168-9.

160   Details of the release of Swedish businessmen are in a letter attributed from Himmler to Kersten, reproduced in Briffault, 149. In September 1943 Hitler grants Himmler's request to commute the prison sentences of the remaining businessmen.

160   "The street is no … only men endure", "The Downfall of Hitler", *The History Place*, 2010, retrieved 16/7/19.

161   "Think, Reichsführer, … German leader", Kessel, 152.

162   Numbers from ibid., 153.

164   *Teppichbeisser*, Michael, loc. 4593 of 5434.

165   Details of Wulff's work in finding Mussolini, Wulff, 85.

165   Details of crayfish party, Briffault, 50.

168   "But you'll … come back?", Kessel, 159.

Chapter V

171   Meeting with Gunther, Kersten, 187.

171   *Durchgeschleust*, Michael loc. 1820 of 5434.

174   "One principle … that is clear", Joel Kovel, "Poetry after the Holocaust", in *Dialectical Anthropology*, vol. 24, no. 3/4, retrieved 16/7/19, https://www.jstor.org/stable/29790607

178   "Dear Reichsführer, … Felix Kersten', Kersten, 190-1.

180   Estimates, ibid., 197.

182   Granting of Extraterritoriality episode, Kessel, 173-4.

184   "How noble … camps", attributed to Kersten, 183.

187   "… paper sheets … Germany", the quote is actually attributed to Kersten, ibid., 185.

188   "You are one … stock?", "Use your greatness … as you can", "I know … cannot", "You must … Danes!", "Ohh … word of this", "Do not think of that", "Very … well". This conversation is reported by Kessel, ibid., 186-7,189.

191   Eventually 7,000 are arrested and of these 4,980 are executed. United States Holocaust Memorial Museum, "The July 20, 1944 Attempt to Assassinate Adolf Hitler", retrieved 16/7/19. https://encyclopedia.ushmm.org/content/en/article/the-july-20-1944-plot-to-assassinate-adolf-hitler

192   "Watch out … the other road", Briffault, 244-5.

192   "All SS … room itself", Peter Longerich, Heinrich Himmler: A Life, retrieved 16/7/19, 343. https://books.google.com.au/books/about/Heinrich_Himmler.html?id=GBQchepZ-7EC 198.

198   Details of those released, Kersten, 230-2.

199   "Dear Reichsführer, … thanks, Felix", ibid., 232.

199   *Werden praktisch*, quoted from Antony Beevor cited by Carlo D'Este, "The Final Days", *New York Times*, 8/9/02, retrieved, 16/7/19. https://www.nytimes.com/2002/09/08/books/the-final-days.html?searchResultPosition=4

200   "Each new train … platform", Beevor, 48.

201   Wulff's view of Kersten, Wulff, 139.

202   Estimates from Train of Commemoration Report, Web Archive, Way Back Machine, "Train of Commemoration Report, Train of Memory",

November 2009, retrieved 16/7/19. http://www.zug-der-erinnerung.eu/
download/gutachten/Gutachten_Vorwort_DE.pdf

204   Based on the translation of a letter by Himmler, Briffault, 228-9.

205   Details of the nurses' tears are from Kessel, 225.

Chapter VI

209   "If we lose … perish with us!", "Yours … thousand people", Kessel,
227. "They shall not … conquerors!", Kersten, 277.

211   "… carcasses of … to death", Wulff, 147.

213   "The concentration camps … Jewish prisoners", Kessel, 230. Kersten
deals with this episode, Kersten, 275-6.

213   "Never in my life … powers of the earth", Kersten, 277.

214   "In the name of humanity", ibid. The Israeli Ambassador confirms this
deal in a letter reproduced, Arno Kersten, 261.

216   "If we are … as well!", Briffault, 258. Kersten was made a Grand
Officer of the Order of Orange-Nassau for his work in helping to
save Dutch nationals, Dutch art treasures, and Dutch cities and
installations from destruction. See https://www.commentarymagazine.
com/articles/the-strange-case-of-himmlers-doctorfelix-kersten-and-count-
bernadotte/

218   "ein absoluter Schwindel", quote and details of Panzerjagd from
Beevor, *Berlin*, 74.

219   Himmler's fear of Hitler shooting him on the spot for meeting with a
Jewish person, Kessel, 232.

219   "Om vi var … ropa", from Luke 19:40. Steven Koblik was the author
of the Swedish Government Report into Sweden's response to the
persecution of the Jews, 1933–45. USHMM, retrieved 16/7/19. https://
collections.ushmm.org/search/catalog/bib6711

221   "A political event … importance", Kersten, 283; "it will be …
miracle", Kessel, 235.

222   Kersten refers to him as "former Austrian Chancellor Seitz", Kersten,
283.

225   Details of those released, from Briffault, 265, 271, 275, 276.

226   "Rejoice … Führer!", Kessel, 237.

228 "I'm afraid Himmler ... made to you", ibid., 238. Details of this discussion between Schellenberg and Kersten, ibid., 238-40 and Kersten, 285.

233 "... bury the hatchet ... the Jews", Kersten, 286. "There is no ... Führer", Briffault, 284.

234 "Crimes ... those camps", attributed to Norbert Masur. "I concede ... responsible", attributed to Himmler, Kersten, 287.

235 "Let us ... still be saved", "At least ... all Jews", ibid.

236 "Above all, ... as Poles", ibid., 289.

239 "We have made ... differently", "Give my greetings ... Auf Wiedersehen", Briffault, 232.

240 "Hitler hears ... his Führer", "The Defeat of Hitler", *The History Place*.

242 "Tell me ... Tell me!", Wulff, 185-6.

246 The Swedish *National Encyclopaedia* puts the numbers saved by the White Buses at a total of 30,000, other sources at 19,000. The White Buses pdf cited on wwwharbourofhope. For information on the Dutch Commission see H. Trevor Roper at: https://www.commentarymagazine. com/articles/the-strange-case-of-himmlers-doctorfelix-kersten-and-count- bernadotte/

253 These numbers are very slippery. The upper figure of 800,000 is from a letter by Moshe Erell (Israeli Ambassador) to Mrs Irmgard Kersten in 1988 and is quoted in Arno Kersten, 161.

Author's note

257 "[h]istory is not ... our own", Professor Julius Lester, quoted in *The Invention of Wings*, Sue Monk Kidd, 423.

258 "... [w]ords have ... becomes apparent", Michael, loc. 89 of 5434.

259 "... [i]n spite ... everything else", Kessel, 16.

259 "just as", Hugh Trevor Roper, ibid., 11.

260 "came back to him", email to author, 18/1/19; "... convinced that ... his hand", email to author, 4/7/19.

261 "There is ... little mystical", Leon Edel in Kiera Lindsey, "Deliberate Freedom: Using Speculation and Imagination in Biography", *Text*, retrieved 16/7/19. http://www.textjournal.com.au/speciss/issue50/ Lindsey.pdf

www.ingramcontent.com/pod-product-compliance
Lightning Source LLC
Chambersburg PA
CBHW032218050726
47591CB00001B/174